Cultivating a Digital Culture for Effective Patient Engagement

A Strategic Framework and Toolkit
for Health-Provider Websites

Cultivating a Digital Culture for Effective Patient Engagement

A Strategic Framework and Toolkit for Health-Provider Websites

Lorren Pettit, MS, MBA

CRC Press
Taylor & Francis Group
Boca Raton   London   New York

CRC Press is an imprint of the
Taylor & Francis Group, an **informa** business

A PRODUCTIVITY PRESS BOOK

CRC Press
Taylor & Francis Group
6000 Broken Sound Parkway NW, Suite 300
Boca Raton, FL 33487-2742

© 2020 by Taylor & Francis Group, LLC
CRC Press is an imprint of Taylor & Francis Group, an Informa business

No claim to original U.S. Government works

Printed on acid-free paper

International Standard Book Number-13: 978-0-367-02435-2 (Hardback)

Library of Congress Cataloging-in-Publication Data

Names: Pettit, Lorren, author.
Title: Cultivating a digital culture for effective patient engagement : a strategic framework and toolkit for health-provider websites / Lorren Pettit.
Description: Boca Raton : Taylor & Francis, 2020. | Includes bibliographical references and index.
Identifiers: LCCN 2019048336 (print) | LCCN 2019048337 (ebook) | ISBN 9780367024352 (hardback ; alk. paper) | ISBN 9780429399657 (ebook)
Subjects: MESH: Health Information Management—methods | Medical Informatics | Marketing of Health Services | Telemedicine | Internet | Patient Participation
Classification: LCC R858 (print) | LCC R858 (ebook) | NLM W 26.5 | DDC 610.285—dc23
LC record available at https://lccn.loc.gov/2019048336
LC ebook record available at https://lccn.loc.gov/2019048337

Visit the Taylor & Francis Web site at
http://www.taylorandfrancis.com

and the CRC Press Web site at
http://www.crcpress.com

Contents

Author

Lorren Pettit, MS, MBA, has been a healthcare executive for more than 30 years, with experience in healthcare operations, corporate planning, and organizational development. Mr. Pettit began his hospital career leading the Geriatric Behavioral Health program for All Saints Health System (now operating as Baylor Scott & White All Saints Medical Center—Fort Worth). Having previously worked for some of the most renown healthcare organizations in the United States, including VHA, Inc. (now operating as Vizient, Inc.), Press Ganey Associates, and HIMSS (Health Information Management and Systems Society), Pettit is currently the CEO and principal of GeroTrend Research, a specialized healthcare market intelligence/consulting firm focused on servicing the clinical competitive positioning performance interests of senior care providers and investors.

Pettit completed his undergraduate work at the University of Winnipeg (Winnipeg, Manitoba, Canada) and achieved a master of science in gerontology from Baylor University (Waco, TX) and a master of business administration from the University of Dallas, Texas. Pettit served for a number of years as an adjunct faculty member at Indiana University, teaching medical sociology, social marketing, and gerontology. Pettit is coauthor of two books, *An Introduction to Health Information Technology in LTPAC Settings* (2018) and *Assessing the Value of Digital Health* (2018).

Chapter 1

Introduction

The Digital Health and Patient Engagement Buzz

The healthcare industry is awash with buzzwords driving market innovations and strategic initiatives. This is evident by perusing most any healthcare publication or walking the exhibit floor of a healthcare trade show. Terms like "Big Data", "Population Health", "Patient Driven Payment Model (PDPM)", and "Patient-Centric" scream out as the next biggest threat or opportunity facing healthcare leaders.

The challenge with "buzzword strategies" is that the leaders of healthcare provider organizations are tempted to chase after the latest and greatest "shiny object" in order to prove their mettle as a progressive leader. Yet, many may have a vague understanding at best of what the idea they are pursuing entails and little to no evidence to support the benefits these ideals will have for their patients and/or organization. This is not to intimate that new and innovative market ideas have little value. Quite the contrary, the explosive growth of innovation inundating the healthcare marketplace is encouraging and should be encouraged. Yet the cautionary note for healthcare leaders in this type of environment is to proceed purposefully by pursuing those strategies that can be supported by evidence.

Two "buzzwords" that have received a lot of interest in healthcare circles over the last few years are *digital health* and *patient engagement*. And for good reason, both ideas have strong evidential support surrounding their impact on positive outcomes for patients and healthcare organizations. Though neither term enjoys a universally accepted definition, there are basic tenets that generally explain what each idea encapsulates.

For the purposes of this book, *digital health* refers to *the wide array of technologies available to healthcare providers and consumers designed to support the health information needs of patients, consumers, and/or providers.* Digital health technologies can range from the wearable fitness trackers capturing patient-generated health data to the electronic health record hospitals employ. Many of these digital tools have functioned to help people gain control over their own lives by providing them with the information they need to make important personal health and wellness decisions.

Though rarely considered as such, the basic premise of this textbook is that provider organizations should consider their consumer/patient facing website as a digital health technology and incorporate their website as part of their digital health strategy. It is after all a digital technology designed to support the health information needs of patients, consumers, and providers. Yet few do despite that almost all healthcare provider organizations of any notable size, have a web presence. While websites across all industries historically functioned as an "electronic brochure" designed to offer the interested basic information about the organization (e.g. services offered, location, contact information), the uses of websites have changed as web tools and consumers have become more sophisticated. This shifting paradigm has not been lost on healthcare provider organizations but is certainly not universally true. Healthcare provider organizations have much room to grow in this area.

The other key buzzword of interest to this textbook, *patient engagement,* refers to *a measurable behavior reflecting a patient's sustained activation and expansion of their empowerment as a patient.* Engaged patients understand their role in the care process; have the knowledge, skill, and confidence to manage their health and healthcare; and demonstrate sustained behaviors pursuing personal health goals. Having engaged patients is a priority many healthcare leaders are pursuing, because the benefits of having patients actively involved in their care are enormous.

To be engaged in one's health though, a patient must be empowered. *Patient Empowerment* is a multidimensional process that helps people gain control over their own lives and increases their capacity to act on issues that they themselves define as important. Empowerment is realized in part when patients have the resources needed to achieve the control desired. As empowerment is not limited to those in a formal/informal relationship with a healthcare professional (e.g. patients), it is perhaps more appropriate to talk about *Health Empowerment.* Health Empowerment is not restricted to the disease model orientation of western medicine, encompassing the broader idea of wellness.

Health Empowerment Web Strategy Index (HEWSi™)

Pulling these two ideas together, the central argument of this book is that healthcare provider organizations can advance the engagement of the populations they serve by purposely leveraging their organization's website as a tool of health empowerment. But to achieve this end, organizations should have a clear understanding of how their website can be used to empower the populations they serve. A framework therefore was needed to articulate how different components of a healthcare provider's website can be leveraged to advance consumers and patients towards the organization's patient engagement goals. The Health Empowerment Web Strategy Index (HEWSi™), presented in the remainder of this textbook, was developed to address this need.

HEWSi™ is both a model and a tool. The HEWSi™ model offers a structural framework for designing a website to empower patients and consumers. This framework is composed of four empowerment domains: *Orienting, Enlightening, Aligning,* and *Personalizing.* These domains lay the foundation for a website's purpose (a.k.a. *function*) by reflecting the expansive health empowerment opportunities and progressive interaction between the provider and website user. Chapters 2–5 detail each of the four domains and include discussion questions at the end of each chapter to help stimulate conversations about the content presented.

Chapter 2 addresses the first and foundational functional domain in the HEWSi™ framework, *Orienting.* Defined as *publicly available information offered by a provider organization designed to introduce and familiarize its targeted audiences (e.g. consumers and patients) to foundational information about the provider organization, Orienting* is arguably the most important and certainly most frequently accessed information on a provider organization's website. *Orienting* consists of eight components:

1. Access
2. Identification
3. Leadership
4. Organizational Story
5. Payment
6. Performance
7. Real-Time
8. Services/Providers

Orienting communication is largely unidirectional, flowing from the provider organization to the website visitor.

The second functional domain, *Enlightening*, is addressed in Chapter 3. *Enlightening* refers to efforts by a provider organization to assist its targeted audiences (e.g. consumers and patients) to associate their individual health interests and experiences with established knowledge and resources. The intent of *Enlightening* is to help foster a deep personal and social understanding about a particular health topic, by aiding website visitors in contextualizing individual health needs/interests to an external resource. The type of information an individual seeks in educating themselves on a health topic of course varies by the specific issue. That said the type of *Enlightening* health content provider organizations place on their website arguably partitions into three categories:

1. Care Environment
2. Clinical
3. Experiential

Though the flow of communication in the *Enlightening* domain is largely unidirectional (from provider organization to website visitor), some aspects of this domain are dynamic as they require a thoughtful input by the website user.

Chapter 4 details the third functional domain *Aligning*. Defined as *website content designed to activate and channel website visitors to pursue some type of behavior supportive of the provider organization's efforts,* the measure of success for *Aligning* is for website visitors to line up their behaviors with those advocated by the provider organization. The flow of communication under the *Aligning* domain is necessarily bidirectional, with opportunities for website visitor-initiated communications more extensive than one would see under the *Orienting* or *Enlightening* domains. While the measure of success in *Aligning* is for the website visitor to take some type of action, not all actions are equally important. Some acts require a greater degree of personal investment than others. *Aligning* recognizes these variances and partitions the demonstrated support into two classes of alignment:

1. Resource Alignment
2. Intimacy

The fourth and final domain of the HEWSi™ model, *Personalizing*, is considered in Chapter 5. *Personalizing* is defined as *content and tools tailored to known individuals made available by a healthcare provider organization in a secure website setting designed to empower an individual patient and/or consumer in realizing their optimal health and wellness goals*. The targeted audience in this domain are not just website visitors, but known patients leveraging the provider's website. Of the domains discussed, *Personalizing* arguably reflects the broadest array of content and tools provider organizations offer users of their website. To harness the varied constituents of this domain into a coherent format, the content and tools under this domain can be collated into the following three components:

1. Empowering Access
2. Empowering Control
3. Optimizing Empowerment

Personalizing represents the healthcare organization's most exacting efforts of leveraging their website as a means of facilitating a digital culture.

Having established the function of the website as a tool to encourage patient engagement, with the domains of the HEWSi™ model designed to progressively advance targeted audiences towards greater and sustained involvement in their care, the discussion in Chapter 6 then turns to the structural aspects, or "form", of the website. Addressing the "form" of the website after detailing the "function" of the website is purposeful. Following the famous axiom that "form follows function", the purpose of the website (its function) informs how the website is to be structured (its form) and therefore must be established first. While the HEWSi™ framework recognizes the importance of the creative design aspects of web designs, the HEWSi™ approach does not address the creative aspects of websites. HEWSi™ is agnostic when it comes to the creative design of a website as the HEWSi™ ideals should apply regardless of the website layout. Website teams looking for guidance on the creative, visual aspects of website design are encouraged to search elsewhere. There are many excellent resources available covering those issues. The discussion in this chapter limits its focus to the following two structural issues:

1. Issues impacting *website users*
2. Issues guiding *content management*

Having laid out the function and the form of the HEWSi™ framework, Chapter 7 of the textbook closes by addressing perhaps the most challenging issues healthcare provider organizations face: how to get patients activated in using the website and tools? How to sustain patient use of the website and tools? Though not an exhaustive treatment of these issues, the discussion here raises the importance of developing and implementing supportive strategies, because building a "killer" website will not be enough in itself to achieve the organization's patient engagement goals.

Chapter 2

Orienting

The Navigational Challenge in Healthcare

Whether we realize it or not, those involved in the delivery of healthcare make an overwhelming number of assumptions about what patients want and, by extension, how accomplished patients are in navigating the healthcare landscape in accessing those things we say they want. Statements like "patients want their health information", "patients want to share in care plan decisions", or "patients want to be empowered and engaged" may not be necessarily wrong, but do presuppose patients have some level of proficiency in traversing the complexities of the healthcare system. The simple fact is, the healthcare ecosystem is confusing and can be overwhelming even to those working within the system, no less those operating with a compromised health status.

The navigational challenges stemming from the physical layout of many hospitals is emblematic of the healthcare industry's long and unflattering history of developing and operating confusing structures. A visit to your local hospital campus will most likely reinforce this point. Given the decentralized way hospitals (and clinics) deliver care today, patients often find themselves navigating through a number of different locations during the course of a single visit. Some have even likened walking around a healthcare facility to a video game with a never-ending series of twists and turns.

To be sure, healthcare leaders do not purposely develop systems and structures to confuse patients. There is a multiplicity of reasons why people have difficulty finding their way around the healthcare ecosystem, like a hospital:

Service Addendums: While most hospitals have had a clear plan when first built, service expansion and increased market demands have required many hospitals to "add-on" to the original structure, thereby compromising the original planner's good intentions.

Complex Service Names: The names of many clinical services are long, difficult to read/pronounce, similar to each other, and frightening to nonclinicians. An individual heading for the Gastroenterological clinic, for example, may follow the signs to the first unit they see with a name beginning with "Gastro" and end up far from where they intended to be.

Patient/User Capabilities: Many patients and visitors have reduced capacities of one kind or another (e.g. visual impairment, reduced mobility, reduced mental capacities, or heightened anxiety) which weaken their wayfinding capabilities.

The navigational challenges of the healthcare ecosystem present a significant and multifaceted concern for patients and healthcare providers alike. Continuing with the challenges associated with the physical layout of hospital campuses for illustrative purposes, the negative impact of "environmentally disoriented" patients can be manifest in a number of ways:

Compromised Patient Outcomes: Patients unable to locate their appointment site or delayed in getting to an appointment may miss receiving prescribed services in a timely fashion. The rescheduling of an appointment places an increased burden on patients to remain engaged in their care plan if they decide to reengage at all. The downstream consequences of *decreased patient engagement/patient compliance* may present in compromised *patient outcomes*.

Decreased Patient Satisfaction/Brand Reputation: Patients who get lost navigating their way through a hospital campus to an appointment, can easily get overwhelmed and frustrated with the situation. While many may initially blame themselves for their inability to find their way around a healthcare campus, they soon redirect their frustration to the organization. The initial decrease in patient satisfaction is difficult for many providers to overcome and can negatively affect the patient's overall perception of the *provider's brand*.

Increased Provider Costs: Patients/visitors who are lost in facilities and ask staff for directions cost the hospital money related to disruptions in staff workflow and productivity. Late or missed appointments can also have a domino effect in delaying/canceling other appointments, increasing the possibility the organization has to pay staff overtime in order to complete delayed procedures or miss revenue opportunities for appointments that did not occur.

To address the navigational challenges presented by campus layouts, savvy healthcare leaders are turning to *wayfinding* research to help inform how to best get patients and visitors to their destinations with ease. Known by a variety of names, "wayfinding" is a multidisciplinary field that pulls liberally from environmental psychology, geography, anthropology, architecture, and environmental design to assist with navigational designs within built environments. Though wayfinding within healthcare facilities has been a task for designers for many decades, it has historically occupied a low organizational priority. This has changed in recent years, as the discipline is recognized as a viable cost-savings tactic for hospital executives and administrators.

Of interest for the present purposes is the recognition that healthcare wayfinding efforts should not be limited to physical campus directions. Patients are like hunters thrust into an expedition they would rather not face. They need as much guidance on how to access their health information or participate in shared care plan decisions, as they do in getting from the hospital's front door to the imaging department. A provider organization's website offers a fantastic medium for orienting *healthcare hunters* to the organization, to include the physical layout of the campus, all of which leads us to the first and foundational functional domain in the Health Empowerment Web Strategy Index (HEWSi™) framework, *Orienting*.

The "Orienting" Domain

Using the term *Orienting*, we mean to refer to *publicly available information offered by a provider organization designed to introduce and familiarize its targeted audiences (e.g. consumers and patients) to foundational information about the provider organization.*

Orienting information allows a provider organization to introduce itself to patients and prospective patients with basic information about the organization, as well as setting the tone for how to navigate the system. It arguably represents some of the most important and certainly most frequently accessed information on a provider organization's website. Though not exclusively limited to what one might find on the "About Us" section of a website, much of what is typically included in an "About Us" web page is orienting information. Some might even characterize a website's orienting information as the organization's "electronic brochure", because *Orienting* is a uniquely unidirectional activity with all communiques flowing from the provider organization to the intended consumer/patient audiences in a publicly accessible format.

The *Orienting* domain is important for several reasons:

Welcomes and Invites: *Orienting* involves the type of information those unfamiliar with the organization most commonly seek first. As such, it represents an entry point for those the organization purposes to serve. Making *Orienting* information available to the public signifies the welcoming of inquiries and serves to invite the intended audiences to learn more about the organization.

Builds Trust/Reduces Anxiety: Recognizing the inherent angst patients often experience when utilizing healthcare services, *Orienting* affords patients the opportunity to acquaint themselves and establish a level of comfort with the organization, before directly utilizing the organization's services.

Organizational Reputation: *Orienting* allows the organization to tell its story and frame its position in the marketplace.

Organizational Culture: Finally, and specific to the purposes of this book, *Orienting* allows the organization to demonstrate the norms and expectations of its use of digital health information. It sets a tone for the organization's digital culture and invites the targeted audiences to embrace the culture for themselves, without presenting itself as exclusive to digital health consumers.

Components of "Orienting"

The type of information an individual seeks in orienting themselves to a topic, organization, event, etc. follows a rudimentary formula known as the *Five-Ws* (sometimes referred to as *Five Ws and How*, *5W1H*, or *Six Ws*). Most frequently associated with the craft of journalists, the Five Ws involve interrogatives (Who, What, Where, When, Why, and How) whose answers are considered basic in information gathering or problem solving. Healthcare organizations can leverage the Five Ws formula as a guide in the development of content for the following eight *Orienting* components:

1. Access: Where/When
2. Identification: Who
3. Leadership: Who
4. Organizational Story: Why
5. Payment: How
6. Performance: How
7. Real-Time: When
8. Services/Providers: What

1. Access

Perhaps the most basic and frequently sought *Orienting* information on a provider's website involves the "where" and "when" of the service delivery. The *where* type of information provided here details the contact points website visitors can use to access the provider organization's services, while the *when* addresses the "time-related" questions website visitors might have about hours of operation and/or timeframes when select activities occur (e.g. visitation hours).

Access is established and reinforced through the following:

Primary Points of Contact: The website includes the provider organization's main contact information.

Primary points of contact include
- Hours of operation and/or visitation hours (if applicable)
- Main fax number (if applicable)
- Main phone number
- Physical address
- Primary email address (for inquiries)

Service Specific Contacts: The website includes contact information for some/all available clinical services.

Service specific contacts may include
- Hours of operation and/or visitation hours (if applicable)
- Main fax number (if applicable)
- Main phone number
- Physical address
- Primary email address (for inquiries)

Wayfinding: The website includes the organization's physical location information.

Wayfinding may include
- A map of the campus in relationship to surrounding area (e.g. cross-streets, local markers)
- An interior map of the health campus
- A statement referencing the provider organization's geographical coverage/area of influence

2. Identification

Identification addresses the "whom does the website represent?" question. Focused on the legal, organizational entity, *Identification* is a significant component of *Orienting* as visitors to a provider's website should be reassured that the content they are viewing is truly representative of the provider organization they intended to access. By clearly asserting their relationship to the website, the provider organization can assure website visitors that the provider organization has reviewed, endorsed, and authorized for publication, the website's content. In doing so, the provider organization is establishing a foundation upon which website visitors/patients can trust that the information presented is information the provider organization intended to share with the public.

Identification can be established and reinforced through the following:

Brand Consistency: The website design reflects the provider organization's brand guidelines.

The messaging as well the appearance of the website reflects the provider organization's brand guidelines such as taglines, font, and color scheme.

Identification Statement: The website includes a statement indicating the provider endorses the website's content.

While organizations may elect to establish *Identification* through a formal statement somewhere on their website, a copyright notice in the footer of each web page achieves the same purpose. Note that as soon as a website is developed, it is automatically copyrighted. Your website copyright gives you exclusive rights to the site's content, and copyright law gives the copyright owner exclusive rights over the following:
- Reproduction of the work
- Preparation of derivative works
- Distribution of copies of the work to the public
- Public display and performance of the work

Example: © 2020 Generic Health System. All Rights Reserved

Name and Logo: The name and/or official logo of the provider organization appears on all main pages of the website.

It is important to have the provider organization's name and/or official logo on all the pages of the website (typically in the web page Header), as it reassures the website user that they continue to remain on the provider's website as they navigate around the website.

Website Uniform Resource Locator (URL): The website's URL reflects the provider organization's corporate name in some form or fashion.

The URL of the website should reflect some (easily) deciphered association to the provider organization's publically referenced facility or corporate name.

Example: www.ghs.mb.ca/ for Generic Health System in Manitoba, Canada

3. Leadership

It is easy to forget when writing a corporate website that people want "connection" with other people. This is especially true in the delivery of healthcare services, where many care sites (e.g. hospitals) have historically triggered a fear response in people. The third *Orienting* component then, *Leadership*, expands on the organizational "who" information by introducing the website visitor to those accountable for the strategic management of the provider organization (e.g. CEO, Chair of the Board). This can be accomplished by simply listing the name of the primary leader or senior leaders of the organization, to including a personal message from the primary leader or publishing a brief biography of each senior leader.

By identifying at least one organizational leader, the provider organization is freeing itself from the confines of projecting its image through an "institutional" screen. Instead, the organization can begin to "humanize" its operation and efforts by leveraging the characteristics of a human emissary. It also signals to website visitors that those leading the organization are unafraid, even proud, to tie their personal reputation to the organization. The personal exposure of this act implies organizational leaders are willing to be accessible and transparent. The vulnerability exhibited through these attributes should help build trust with those using the provider organization's services and possibly reduce patient anxiety.

Leadership can be established and reinforced through the following:

Leadership Team: The website includes a listing of the various leaders of the organization and their role/function (usually the Executive Team).

Leadership Team Profile: The website includes a biographic profile of the leaders of the organization.

The profiles profile the leaders of the organization beyond the primary leader (e.g. CEO).

Primary Leader: The website publishes the name of the organization's primary leader (e.g. CEO, Board Chairperson).

Given that we live in a visual world, a picture of the primary leader should accompany the name in order to direct website visitor's attention to the primary leader's name.

Primary Leader Message: The website publishes a welcome message from the primary leader to web visitors.

These notes should avoid "flowery" language as it comes across as contrived or worse, fake. Candor, on the other hand, is compelling as web visitors more often than not, appreciate the honesty.

Example: Welcome to the Generic Health System website. Thank you for choosing the hospital closest to where you live and work as the provider for your health care. We are committed to providing the highest quality patient care in a friendly, compassionate setting.

It is valuable to know that when it comes to getting the best help in the shortest amount of time, you don't have far to go. We're here to help you get well, get healthy, and get your life back to normal as quickly as possible. Our mission is to provide compassionate, lifelong healthcare to the individual, family, and community. This means that in everything we do, our focus is on you. We consider it a privilege to serve you.

We hope that you will visit our website often for easy access to the most up-to-date information about the many services and medical specialties available for you and your family at Generic Health System. Please stop by and visit our facility when you are in the area. If you have questions or comments, please let us know.

Sincerely,
xxxxxxx, CEO
Generic Health System

Primary Leader Profile: The website includes a biographic profile of the organization's primary leader.

A biographic profile of the organization's primary leader is published to include, at the very least, a summary of their professional self (e.g. education, work experience). A more intimate profile reflects personal information (e.g. hobbies, family life).

4. Organizational Story

Orienting affords organizations the opportunity to tell web visitors why the organization exists. Referred to as the *organizational story*, the "why" question here touches on what the organization purposes to achieve as well as the corporate values guiding its efforts. Many organizations choose to share this information from an objective third-party stand-point. The focus on facts and the neutrality reflective of this approach can present as somewhat sterile but does work to reinforce the clinical nature of the organization. A growing number of organizations though are shunning the "corporate resume" approach, believing many in their intended audience view corporate-speak as boring, stiff, and insincere. While facts are important, the passion surrounding the company's story can be lost when discussed in a matter-of-fact manner. As stories tend to be much more memorable than facts, many provider organizations are beginning to adopt a much more conversational style in telling the organization's raison d'être. Organizations can still appear as professional while being casual, even humorous, when talking about the organization.

Organizational Story is established and reinforced through the following:

Mission, Vision, and Values: The website includes the provider organization's mission and vision statements and key values.

Mission and vision both relate to an organization's purpose. A mission statement communicates the organization's reason for being as well as how it aims to serve its key stakeholders. A vision statement is a future-oriented pronouncement of the organization's aspirations. Values are the emotionally invested principles guiding the organization in realizing their mission and vision.

Organization History and Milestones: The website includes a summary profile of the organization's history and key moments.

Many healthcare provider organizations have a rich history of supporting the communities they serve. This information can be very helpful to website users looking to establish a relationship with a community provider.

5. Payment

A critical topic under the *Orienting* umbrella involves "how" patients can pay for the services rendered. While *Payment* information will vary significantly by country as well as the type of service covered, all provider organizations have some type of expectation regarding a patient's financial obligations. *Payment* information covers general patient financial information and explains *how* patients can pay for the services utilized (e.g. insurance accepted), as well as access financial support services. *Payment* is a significant topic area to address in the *Orienting* section because the confusion associated with patient billing practices (at least in the United States) can be a huge source of frustration for patients.

Payment is established and reinforced through the following:

Payment Process: The website includes an overview of the payment process.

Informing patients, even at a high level, about how the payment for clinical services works, can alleviate a tremendous amount of their stress.

Example: Your type of insurance will determine the timing of your bill. Typically, we send you a bill after your insurance company has processed the bill. There might be times when your insurance has not responded to our request for payment, and we may ask you to become involved in resolving the open balance.

Payment Resources: The website provides users with contact information for those with payment questions/concerns.

Recognizing the confusion patient bills can generate as well as the inability of some patients to pay for services rendered, the website provides users with contact information for those with payment questions/concerns.

Example: If you have any questions about your health coverage, it is best to contact your employer/plan administrator or the insurance carrier directly. For more information, contact the Business Office Call Center by phone at xxx-xxx-xxxx or by email at xxxx@xxxxxxx.xxx.

Payment Responsibilities: The website includes a statement regarding patient responsibility in paying for the services rendered.

It is important that before services are rendered, patients have an understanding of what expectations the provider organization has of patients regarding their responsibilities in paying for healthcare services.

Example: When you are scheduled for a doctor's appointment or other test, study, or procedure at xxxx Hospital, the representative who checks you in will enter the information needed for your patient chart, and to help us bill your insurance. At this time, we will discuss your portion of the financial responsibility. We will let you know how much your copay and deductible will be for the service we will be providing.

Payment Sources: The various payment sources accepted by the provider organization are listed.

Though the type of payment sources included in this section will vary greatly by country, there should be some explanation as to the varied payment sources the provider accepts.

6. Performance

The sixth *Orienting* information considered in this chapter, performance, involves "how" related questions: "How well does the provider organization perform its service?" and "How is the provider organization working to improve and/or maintain a high level of performance?" The healthcare provider industry is awash with publicly reported performance measures and recognition programs. Governments and insurance carriers mandate some of these measures, while others stem from voluntary performance measurement activities. This information is valuable to consumers on two fronts. First, public performance measures and recognition programs can help consumers select (if consumers have a choice at all) which provider to use for a certain service. Second, performance transparency reassures consumers that provider organizations are motivated and energized to improve or maintain high levels of performance. Despite commonly cited concerns over the limitations, validity, and interpretability of some of these publicly reported measures, the heightened awareness of the data can work to intensify the provider organization's focus on performance improvement activities.

While fragments of a provider organization's publicly reported performance can be pieced together from a dizzying array of websites, the *Orientating performance* information of interest here surrounds the coalescing of this information on the provider organization's website. By collating and displaying the information on the website, the provider organization makes it easier for its target audiences to adjudicate for themselves how well the provider organization performs its service.

Performance is established and reinforced through the following:

Clinical Quality: The website contains some level of detail on the provider organization's clinical performance.

> While the provider organization has full discretion on the selection of the clinical areas and measures used to reflect the organization's clinical performance, the most recent information displayed should be no more than 1 year old. The information supplied should include an explanation of the measurement methodology.

Community Involvement: The website profiles the organization's assessment of and/or involvement in supporting the care needs of at-risk communities.

> The provider organization provides some level of information on their civic *performance* (e.g. development of a community needs assessment/plan, charity care expenditures, involvement in community activities).

Complaints: The website explains how users can register a complaint about the organization's services.

As a provider of a service, complaints and grievances from those using the organization's services are bound to occur. To get ahead of this, the provider organization should detail how individuals can register complaints and grievances about the organization to some oversight body (albeit through an internal process or an external entity).

External Recognition: The website identifies the organization's various externally assessed awards/certifications.

Healthcare organizations work hard to offer high-quality services to the communities they serve. These efforts are not unnoticed by varied external industry stakeholders. As a result, numerous award programs exist to recognize the efforts of healthcare organizations. Organizational leaders can leverage these recognition programs to enhance the morale of the staff involved in achieving the awards, as well as using the recognition program to promote the organization to its targeted audiences.

Patient Satisfaction: The provider organization publishes their most current patient satisfaction indicators, to include an explanation of the data collection/analysis approach.

Patient satisfaction is a valuable measure many organizations have been monitoring for several years now. The presentation of these scores can aid website in their decision to select one provider organization over another.

Performance Improvement: The provider organization provides some level of information on efforts to improve their services.

Healthcare provider organizations are challenged by many internal and external forces to continually improve their clinical performance. Sharing the organization's performance improvement efforts with web users is a valued way to publicly reinforce the organization's commitment to providing high-quality care to the community it serves.

7. Real-Time Informing

The *real-time informing* information supports efforts to address the "when" questions website visitors might have about accessing the provider organization's services. The type of information provided here provides website visitors real-time information about the organization, such as the current wait time in the Emergency Department. This information helps set service expectations for patients choosing to use the organization's services at that moment, as well as allowing them the opportunity to select another healthcare provider organization's services if the service expectation does not satisfy their needs/wants.

Real-time informing is established and reinforced through the following:

Current Wait-Time Counter: The website provides the current average wait time for select clinical services (e.g. Emergency Department, Urgent Care).

Webcam: The website provides a real-time video feed of select areas of the campus (e.g. parking lot) to help prepare patients when accessing the organization's services.

8. Services/Providers

A provider organization's core business arguably partitions into two parts:

Clinical Services: The array of medical services related to the actual observation and treatment of patients, available through the provider organization.

Clinicians: The healthcare provider(s) (e.g. physicians, nurse practitioners, occupational therapists) with a formal association (e.g. admitting privileges, employed by the organization) to the provider organization.

The *Services/Providers* information purposes to identify and detail key elements of the organization's primary business by addressing the "what" of the provider organization: "What type of clinical services does the provider organization offer?" and "What is known about the clinicians practicing at the provider organization?"

Services/Providers is established and reinforced through the following:

Clinical Practitioner Directory: The website lists the clinical practitioners formally associated with the provider organization.

Here again, the challenge for provider organizations is how to best present this list, alphabetical name, searchable by name/location, specialty, etc.

Clinical Practitioner Profile: The website provides some level of information on the clinical practitioner(s) associated with the organization.

The profile should include professional-associated information (e.g. schools attended, board certifications) but may also extend into personal facts (e.g. interests, hobbies).

Clinical Services Description: The website provides some level of detail explaining and/or describing the clinical services available at the provider organization.

Offering a brief explanation of the selected clinical service can help the website visitor better understand the services accessed.

Clinical Services Directory: The website lists the clinical services available at the provider organization.

The challenge for most organizations is how to best present clinical services to a nonclinical audience. The names of clinical services and departments like *Otolaryngology* can be intimidating to the novice. A more simplistic presentation of the same service, *Ear, Nose, and Throat*, would better serve the intended audience.

One way to organize the clinical services directory is to map a patients' journey to and through a provider organization's services. Patients visiting a hospital website postdiagnosis, for example, are likely to navigate through the website based on the care offered by condition or disease. An easy way to get started in developing a patient journey map is to ask a few powerful questions:

– What does the patient know about her condition/health need?
– What should the patient know about his or her condition/health need?

- What is the patient feeling right now?
- How would the patient like to feel?
- How might the patient seek answers and solutions to her condition/ health need?
- What are the possible touch points the patient might experience with our brand along her journey?

Summary

The healthcare ecosystem can be confusing and overwhelming to those operating with a compromised health status. Patients need guidance on how to navigate through the complex web of care. A provider organization's website presents a fantastic medium for introducing itself to patients and prospective patients with basic information about the organization, as well as setting the tone for how to navigate the system.

Referred to here as *Orienting*, this type of information arguably represents some of the most important and certainly most frequently accessed information on a provider organization's website. There are eight categories of *Orienting* content information healthcare organizations should publish on their website:

1. Identification: *whom does the website represent?*
2. Leadership: *who is in charge of the organization?*
3. Services/Providers: *what type of services does the organization offer?*
4. Access: *where is the organization located? When can services be assessed?*
5. Real-Time Informing: *when can patients be seen?*
6. Organizational Story: *why does the organization do what it does?*
7. Payment: *how can patients pay for the services rendered?*
8. Performance: *how well does the provider organization perform its service?*

Discussion Questions

1. How does *Orienting* support a provider organization's digital culture?
2. Which one of the *Orienting* components do you consider most important to the following audiences? Explain your answer.
   a. Prospective patients
   b. Current patients
   c. Vendors selling clinical products to the organization
3. The challenge many provider organizations have with publishing a Clinical Services Directory is how to present clinical services to a non-clinical audience. Discuss a provider website that you believe did a good job in presenting their clinical services to a nonclinical audience.
4. How might the posting of "unflattering" clinical performance scores benefit a provider organization? The provider organization's website visitors?

Chapter 3

Enlightening

Contextualizing Personal Health

In the previous chapter, the *Orienting* domain was introduced to provide website visitors with basic knowledge about the provider organization, as well as set a tone for how one navigates through the provider's system. The informational grounding that *Orienting* establishes for first time website visitors is critical, whether they be healthcare provider novices or experienced patients. It allows them to adjudicate the provider organization as a resource in addressing their personal health needs and interests. Based on this orientation, website visitors either flag the site as a potentially valuable resource requiring further exploration, or not. It is incumbent on provider organizations then to ensure the primary entry point(s) of the website capture the orientation needs and interests of the audience(s) the provider organization intends to attract, and activate them to learn more of the particular issue that drove them to visit the website in the first place. Clearly addressing the Five Ws of *Orienting* is critical in this process.

Once the interest of a website visitor is activated, there are a multiplicity of ways the user might want to leverage the provider organization's website as a resource. Arguably, one of the paths that moves the patient closer to being engaged in their care involves information surrounding personal health concerns. Patients are often motivated to seek reassurances from formal health institutions (albeit a physician or a provider organization's website) that their personal health needs and interests are not only shared by others but that a course of action exists to remedy their concerns. Website visitors reflecting these drivers are looking to contextualize their isolated personal health experiences by attempting to gain a deeper level of understanding and insight on the health topic of interest. To exploit the website visitor's demand for validation, a provider organization's website should include content designed to educate and motivate the validation seeker.

The "Enlightening" Domain

Enlightening, the second functional domain in the Health Empowerment Web Strategy Index (HEWSi™) framework, refers to *efforts by a provider organization to assist its targeted audiences (e.g. consumers and patients) to associate their individual health interests and experiences with established knowledge and resources, with the intent of fostering a deep personal and social understanding about a particular health topic.* It aids website visitors in contextualizing individual health needs/interests to an external resource. Though the flow of communication in the *Enlightening* domain is largely unidirectional (from provider organization to website visitor), some aspects of this domain are dynamic as they require thoughtful input by the website user.

Educating website visitors, a valuable mediating step towards engaging patients in their care, constitutes a significant function of the *Enlightening* domain. Educating website visitors (as well as prospective and current patients) is important for a multiplicity of reasons. Chief among these is that education helps patients make informed decisions. One of the primary goals of patient-centered care is integrating patients as partners in the care team. In order to make this partnership work successfully, providers must account for patient preferences. Ensuring informed shared decision-making relies heavily on patient education efforts. When patients are more knowledgeable about their care and potential treatment options, they are better able to identify how they want (or do not want) to receive healthcare services.

Components of "Enlightening"

The type of information an individual seeks in educating themselves on a health topic of course varies by the specific issue. That said, the type of *Enlightening* health content provider organizations place on their website arguably partitions into three categories:

1. Care environment
2. Clinical
3. Experiential

1. Care Environment

The *care environment* constitutes a significant body of health knowledge which website visitors may expect provider organizations to publish on their websites. In the current context, *care environment* refers to *the physical and social characteristics of a geographically defined setting, which exert some type of influence on the way a healthcare service is accessed/delivered.* Understanding the care environment is a crucial step towards patient engagement as it helps contextualize for the patient some of the processes involved in the delivery of care. Recognizing that some healthcare processes do not make sense (e.g. why do some provider organizations require patients to fill out multiple forms that ask the same question), addressing these concerns (e.g. the adoption of health IT will reduce inefficient intake redundancies) may lead to better patient compliance.

Care environment enlightenment can be established and reinforced through the following:

Advanced Clinical Services Description: The website provides a more than cursory description of the clinical services offered by the provider organization.

This education resource is the most localized of the *care environment* resources as it focuses exclusively on the services of the provider organization. Intimately linked to the *clinical service description* presented under *Orienting*, the description offered expands on the high-level summary used for orientation purposes. The intent is to address the more detailed questions website visitors might have of select clinical services. Given variances in the audiences provider organizations may be targeting, there is no standard for what constitutes an "advanced description". The information presented here can work to help position the provider organization as a "high-tech" organization.

Example: The Robotic Surgery at Generic Children's Hospital is one of the only hospitals in the state to perform Pediatric

Ureteral Reimplantation Surgery using the Brand Name Robotic Surgical System. The minimization of trauma, incision size, and the resulting scarring are significant advantages provided by a less invasive surgical approach. The Brand Name System provides further advantages of a motion scaling and tremor reduction that are critical in work in and around the small anatomical structures of infants and children.

Children's hospitals throughout the world are successfully integrating robotics into their practice, allowing them to perform better surgery and extend the benefits of minimally invasive procedures to children and their families.

Patient Benefits

- Shorter hospital stays
- Less postoperative pain
- Less risk of infection
- Less blood loss and need for transfusions
- Less scarring and improved cosmesis
- Faster recovery and quicker return to normal activities

Fast Facts about Ureteral Reimplantation Surgery

- Ureteral Reimplantation is a surgery to fix the tubes that connect the bladder to the kidneys.
- The surgery changes the position of the tubes at the point where they join the bladder to stop urine from backing up into the kidneys.
- Your child's surgery will be done under general anesthesia, which means that he or she will be sound asleep during the surgery.
- In addition to the general anesthesia, your child may receive caudal anesthesia, which will give pain relief in the area below the waist.
- A pediatric urology surgeon—a doctor who specializes in conditions of the urinary tracts and reproductive organs of children—will do your child's Ureteral Reimplantation surgery.
- Your child will stay in the hospital for 1–2 days after this surgery.

What Is Ureteral Reimplantation?

Ureteral Reimplantation is used to treat reflux (REE-flux), a condition in which urine from the bladder can flow back up into the kidneys through the tubes that connect the kidneys with the bladder.

- ■ When these tubes, called the ureters, are working properly, urine flows only one way out through them from the kidneys and into the bladder so that it can leave the body. The ureters connect to the bladder through a tunnel that acts as a valve to keep urine from flowing backward.
- ■ Sometimes, a ureter has a bad connection to the bladder wall. When there is not enough of the tunnel at the connection point, reflux will occur. If left untreated, reflux can cause scarring of the kidneys and permanent kidney damage.
- ■ When reflux is not expected to go away with time, or is causing kidney damage, surgery is needed.
- ■ Surgery to correct reflux consists of changing the way the ureter connects to the bladder by creating a new tunnel into the bladder. The doctor "reimplants" the ureter to fix its connection to the bladder.

Community/Social Services Directory: The website provides a listing of local health/social service organizations and events.

This type of educational resource focuses on the community within which the provider organization operates. The intent of this content information is to expose website visitors to local health-related resources (e.g. events, activities, organizations) that complement the provider organization's efforts. The community-related information the provider organization should publish involves the following:

Supportive (nonurgent) community resources (e.g. addiction counseling, transportation services) to include relevant contact information

Community health events (e.g. education classes, screenings)

Community resource to address urgent/sensitive health issues (e.g. suicide, domestic violence) to include relevant contact information

Local/National/International Health News: The website provides access to a health news resource by redirecting web users to an external news source or pulling news stories into the website.

This education resource is the most globalized of the *care environment* resources. The intent of this content information is to expose website visitors to factors from the larger healthcare ecosystem that may have some impact on the provider organization's efforts.

RSS (Really Simple Syndication) is an easy way for a provider organization to feed current news stories to their website. Below are some of the more popular healthcare RSS feeds:

1. Modern Healthcare | The leader in healthcare business news, research & data
2. *Healthcare Design Magazine* (HCD) | Industry News, Trends & Projects
3. Healthcare IT News
4. TEDMED Blog
5. Healthcare Economist
6. The Health Care Blog
7. *Healthcare Informatics Magazine* | Health IT
8. HHS Blog | The U.S. Department of Health and Human Services
9. Healthcare.gov—Health Insurance Blog
10. MedCity News—Healthcare technology news, life science current events
11. HealthITSecurity.com
12. Medical Dialogues—Medical Professionals & Healthcare News
13. HIT Consultant—Healthcare IT News
14. HealthITAnalytics
15. Healthcare Success
16. The Hill: Healthwatch
17. Healthcare—Cisco Blog
18. Health | The Atlantic
19. Safe Healthcare Blog | Centers for Disease Control and Prevention
20. Global Health Portal | Northwestern University
21. Deloitte Center for Health Solutions
22. Experian Healthcare Blog
23. Bloomberg BNA | Health Care Blog
24. The Henry J. Kaiser Family Foundation
25. Beckers Hospital Review
26. Kaiser Health News
27. Health IT Buzz
28. Manipal Hospitals | Healthcare Blog
29. StaffNurse

30. Isabel Healthcare Blog
31. GPonline | Daily medical, primary care & healthcare news
32. Healthcare Dive | Healthcare and Health IT News
33. Adventist HealthCare & You
34. Agfa HealthCare | eHealth & Digital Imaging
35. The Kindred Continuum
36. UVM Medical Center Blog
37. Spok's Mobility in Healthcare Blog
38. HIStalk
39. Healthcare Australia News
40. Healthy Debate
41. Cambia Health Solution | Health Care Blog
42. The Red Ribbon Blog—Weatherby Healthcare
43. HEALTHCARE First
44. Home Health Care News
45. Practice Builders—Medical Healthcare Marketing
46. Healthcare IT Leaders
47. MaxCure Hospitals
48. VitreosHealth Blog
49. Day Pitney Healthcare Law Blog
50. NHE | The Scalpel's Daily Blog
51. Health Care Law Today | Healthcare Industry News | Foley & Lardner
52. Notes Read
53. Behavioral Healthcare Magazine
54. Hospital Management—Healthcare Industry News
55. Verscend Blog | Healthcare Analytics
56. HPN Online
57. Health Care News
58. HealthcareLink Blog
59. Health Populi
60. CuroMe
61. Health Care For All
62. Healthcare Asia—Medical and healthcare news in Asia
63. Life as a Healthcare CIO
64. *Health Care in India*—Your Health Newspaper
65. Scepticemia
66. iPatientCare
67. HCLDR | Healthcare Leadership Blog

68. Renown Health
69. HCO News—Healthcare Construction & Operations
70. *The Journal of Healthcare Contracting*
71. Health Business Blog
72. Care And Cost | Health Care Essays by Brian Klepper
73. Health Care Policy and Marketplace Review
74. EOS Surfaces
75. Easy Pay Patient Payments Blog
76. Healthcare Exchange Standards
77. Health Care Conversation | Optum
78. Christina's Considerations
79. *Australian Hospital & Healthcare Bulletin*
80. World Health Care Blog
81. Healthcare Standards
82. Update Medicine
83. YouCare
84. Health Care for All New York
85. Health Care Renewal
86. Healthcare IT Experts Blog
87. HealthMatters | UK Healthcare Blog
88. Sheppard Mullin | Healthcare Law Blog
89. Future Patient—Musings on patient-led healthcare
90. Focus Integrative Healthcare Blog
91. Blog About Healthcare | Medical topics relating to healthcare & medicine in the UK
92. The Healthcare Data, Technology & Services Blog
93. AB Hospitals | Smart Surgery Centres Blog
94. World Health Forum Blog
95. Rickard & Associates Healthcare Blog
96. Get Ready | American Public Health Association
97. Gwinnett Medical
98. Health Care Law Blog | Arent Fox

2. Clinical

Clinical education constitutes a key topic area under enlightenment. This should come as no surprise as a provider organization's core business, albeit a hospital, dentist office, or nutrition center, centers on the observation and treatment of patients. Website visitors would understandably seek to advance their understanding of clinical issues then, from an organization that purports to treat the ailments they report to have.

Clinical enlightenment can be established and reinforced through the following:

Complimentary/Alternative Medicine (CAM): The website provides information related to CAM.

Though Allopathic medicine (also called orthodox medicine, conventional medicine, scientific, or Western medicine) is the dominant medical approach used in most developed countries to treat disease and illness, there has been an increased awareness and interest from both public and governmental sectors in CAM. Given the growing demand for CAM in Western markets, it is valuable to spend some time providing a brief overview of this segment of the healthcare ecosystem.

Frequently referenced as one big category, complementary medicine differs from alternative medicine in that complementary medicine is used alongside conventional medicine when there is some degree of scientific evidence to suggest the intervention is safe and effective. Alternative medicine, on the other hand, is used in place of conventional therapies. CAM covers a wide range of disciplines, most of which are guided by the "healing model" of holistic medicine. This model emphasizes the complex interplay between multiple factors: biochemical, environmental, psychological, and spiritual.

CAM involves a diverse group of therapies and interventions that are frequently grouped into overlapping categories:

Mind–Body Medicine uses a range of techniques to help boost the mind's ability to influence bodily functions and symptoms.

Examples: biofeedback, deep relaxation, guided imagery, hypnotherapy, meditation, prayer, support groups, and yoga

Biological Medicine uses substances found in nature, such as foods, herbs, and vitamins to promote health.

Manipulative and Body-Based Methods (a.k.a. Manual Medicine) use manipulation and/or movement of one or more parts of the body to impact one's health.

Examples: chiropractic, massage, osteopathy, physical therapy, and reflexology

Energy Medicine involves the use of body energy fields to promote health. Some forms of energy medicine are designed to influence energy fields believed by some to surround and penetrate the human body. The energy therapy approaches present as the most "mystical" of the CAM categories and are the hardest approaches for conventional medicine to accept.

> *Examples*: qi gong, Reiki, therapeutic touch, electroacupuncture

Despite the above variances, CAM approaches tend to have the following commonalities:

Holism: In holistic medicine both the organism and the disease are frequently looked upon as whole and complete entities, and analysis begins from this perspective rather than from the parts or details. This has often been called "energetics" in modern holistic practice.

The involvement of the mind, body, and soul: While many conventional medicine clinicians acknowledge the importance of the mind–body connection, CAM practitioners place a great emphasis on this relationship and generally never treat one without the other.

The possibility of high-level wellness: In CAM, health is viewed from a positive perspective. It is not the absence of symptoms or clinical disease, but an orientation that dominates conventional medicine. Rather, it is viewed as being a very positive physical–emotional state.

Vitalism: Vitalism is the concept that the living body is animated by a spiritual or nonmaterial agency that marks the true difference between life and death. It contends that living organisms are fundamentally different from nonliving entities because they contain some nonphysical element or are governed by different principles than are inanimate things. Vitalism is often referred to as the "vital spark" or "energy" that some equate with the soul.

The healing processes: Finally, CAM operates from the premise that healer and patient both have a role in the healing process. For the CAM worker, the mindset is one in which they work "with" instead of "on" patients. This shift in thinking is significant as it comes to developing treatment plans.

Over the years, there has been an "uneasy" relationship between CAM and scientific medicine. For those representing conventional medicine, the concerns around CAM fall into three major buckets:

1. There is no scientific basis for the interventions, and the interventions are therefore considered to be worthless at best and potentially dangerous at worst.
2. Since CAM is thought to be worthless, CAM followers are considered to be fooled into thinking that the interventions will help them. The concern here is that people are placing their hope in "mystical" things when they could be getting better if they would only pursue more proven approaches.
3. CAM competes with orthodox medicine. This can be a threat to orthodox medicine's best interest; therefore, it is better to diminish the competition than support it.

CAM advocates also have concerns about scientific medicine. These concerns fall into two major camps:

1. Orthodox medicine is thought to have failed or even harmed some people. It is not that scientific medicine does not benefit people, but the CAM advocates reject the "one-size-fits-all" approach that scientific medicine tends to hold.
2. Scientific medicine tends to position itself as the only viable approach. Because it is grounded in "science", its "true effectiveness" requires the direction of a scientist (a.k.a. physician). Taken together, these factors create a situation where the input of the patient tends to be diminished in favor of the physician. As a result, patient choice in seeking nonconventional interventions is limited.

Despite the tense relationship between CAM and conventional medicine, an increasingly knowledgeable patient population is fueling the CAM movement by seeking alternatives to traditional treatments. Whereas just a few decades ago, alternative therapies were readily dismissed by physicians as fringe medicine, today CAM is earning the attention and respect of conventional medical institutions. The National Institute for Health (NIH), for example, has recognized the need for a CAM division: the National Center for Complementary and Alternative Medicine (NCCAM). CAM is even being embraced (albeit slowly) by conventional academic institutions. Approximately two-thirds of medical schools reportedly offer at least one CAM course to their medical students.

With the growing institutional acceptance of CAM, it should come as no surprise that visitors to provider organization websites would expect provider organizations to address the role CAM has in the organization. Some of the more widely accepted CAM providers and/or interventions provider organizations may want to consider addressing on their website follow:

Chiropractic: A chiropractic is a healthcare profession that focuses on the relationship between the body's structure, mainly the spine, and its functioning. Although practitioners may use a variety of treatment approaches, they primarily perform adjustments (manipulations) to the spine or other parts of the body with the goal of correcting alignment problems, alleviating pain, improving function, and supporting the body's natural ability to heal itself.

The term "chiropractic" combines the Greek words *cheir* (hand) and *praxis* (practice) to describe a treatment done by hand. Hands-on therapy—especially adjustment of the spine—is central to chiropractic care. Chiropractic is based on the notion that the relationship between the body's structure (primarily that of the spine) and its function (as coordinated by the nervous system) affects health.

Spinal adjustment/manipulation is a core treatment in chiropractic care, but it is not synonymous with chiropractic. Chiropractors commonly use other treatments in addition to spinal manipulation, and other healthcare providers (e.g., physical therapists or some osteopathic physicians) may use spinal manipulation.

Chiropractic as an intervention is fully recognized in all 50 states. Chiropractic colleges accredited by the Council on Chiropractic Education (CCE) offer Doctor of Chiropractic (D.C.) degree programs. (CCE is the agency certified by the U.S. Department of Education to accredit chiropractic colleges in the United States.) Admission to a chiropractic college requires a minimum of 90 semester hour credits of undergraduate study, mostly in the sciences.

Chiropractic professionals are regulated individually by each state and the District of Columbia. All states require completion of a D.C. degree program from a CCE-accredited college. Examinations administered by the National Board of Chiropractic Examiners are required for licensing and include a mock patient encounter. Most states require chiropractors to earn annual continuing education credits to maintain their licenses. Chiropractors' scope of practice varies by state in areas such as the dispensing or selling of dietary supplements and the use of other complementary health practices such as acupuncture.

Acupuncture: The term "acupuncture" describes a family of procedures involving the stimulation of points on the body using a variety of techniques. The acupuncture technique that has been most often studied scientifically involves penetrating the skin with thin, solid, metallic needles that are manipulated by the hands or by electrical stimulation. Practiced in China and other Asian countries for thousands of years, acupuncture is one of the key components of traditional Chinese medicine, where the intervention was designed to balance "yin and yang" and assure flow of one's vital energy (chi). Acupuncture became better known in the United States in 1971, when *New York Times* reporter James Reston wrote about how doctors in China used needles to ease his pain after surgery. American practices of acupuncture incorporate medical traditions from China, Japan, Korea, and other countries.

The primary goal of acupuncture is to restore internal balance. That is, balance between the human being and one's environment. Interesting in that when you think back earlier in this course when we were talking about the history of medicine, this was the same idea that drove Hypocrites' thinking. Although millions of Americans use acupuncture each year, often for chronic pain, there has been considerable controversy surrounding its value as a therapy and whether it is anything more than placebo. Research exploring several possible mechanisms for acupuncture's pain-relieving effects is ongoing.

Spiritual Healing: A major area addressed by religion/spirituality is the question of suffering, which is often related to how illness, dying, death, and life beyond death are understood. Most religious/spiritual traditions include healing as a key aspect, whether through prayer, laying on of hands, ritual, and/or other practices. In some cases, healing refers to the expectation that the person who is sick will be fully cured. In other cases, it involves healing on a deeper level that may or may not correspond to a "cure". Indeed, in some cases, full healing may be thought to take place only after death.

Faith is a key component of any spiritual healing intervention. Depending on the spiritual basis of the belief system, this faith…

- Activates innate recuperative forces within
- Transfers healing energy to the patient
- Provides a conduit for cosmic energy, or
- Provide a conduit for spirits and God

In the Christian faith, spiritual healing is most commonly manifest through prayer and ritual, as well as the laying on of hands.

Prayer for the sick or *intercessional prayer* is classified as a paranormal phenomenon. A cleric or layperson, sometimes a small group or congregation, offers prayers to a higher power in order to bring about individual healing. In the Christian church, we see a pattern for prayer in the New Testament, James 5: 14–15.

Closely related to prayers for the sick, the *laying on of hands* involves the act of touching the patient while prayers for healing are offered to a higher power. The practice can be led by a cleric who acts as an intermediary between the higher power and the patient. However, in certain groups, such as charismatic Christians, many people may lay their hands on the patient. The pattern for the laying on of hands in the Christian church is grounded on a passage in the New Testament, Mark 16: 17–18.

Most of the evidence in support of spiritual healing comes from the stories and experiences of strong believers. Western medicine has no explanation for the miraculous healing that is sometimes reported. However, this practice has become the subject of serious clinical research.

Ethnic folk healing practices: Healing practices grounded in the beliefs and practices of cultural groups also fall under the CAM heading. The two most notable ethnic healing practices in North America come from the Mexican American Indians and the Native American Indians.

Curanderism: A Curandero is a traditional healer or shaman which has its roots among the Mexican Indians. Curanderism is conceptually holistic in nature; no separation is made between mind and body, yet use God's will to cure their patients. The techniques include herbs, midwifery, massage, and spiritual techniques. While Curanderism is most common in Mexico and other Latin

American countries, the migration of peoples into the U.S. has spurred the growth of Curanderos in "northern"-tier cities in the United States.

Native American Healing: Native American healing is a broad term that includes healing beliefs and practices of hundreds of indigenous tribes of North America. It combines religion, spirituality, herbal medicine, and rituals used to treat people with medical and emotional conditions. Native American healing is grounded in a belief that all things are interrelated at and that everything lives in an ordered system. The role of the "medicine man" or "medicine woman" (English terms used to describe traditional healers and spiritual leaders among Native American and other indigenous or aboriginal peoples) is to appease the spirits to bring about harmony and order.

Generalized Clinical Information: The website provides access to generalized clinical information related to various pathological conditions.

Note there is no suggestion that the clinical information presented on the website is to be exhaustive, nor that the provider organization is to be responsible for populating the website with this type of information. A plurality of consumer-friendly health specific websites already exists offering information on disorders and conditions, diagnoses and treatments, etc. The charge here is for provider organizations to facilitate website visitors in accessing basic information about the clinical issues the provider organization addresses. If a provider organization elects to depend on a third party for generalized clinical information by redirecting web visitors to an external URL address, the provider organization should alert the visitor that they would be leaving the provider organization's website. Provider organizations should also include some type of statement, noting the provider organization's dependence on third-party content and the provider organization's stance on the endorsement of the content.

Example (Standard Disclaimer for External Links)
These links are being provided as a convenience and for informational purposes only; they do not constitute an endorsement or an approval by the Library of Congress of any of the

products, services, or opinions of the corporation or organization or individual. The Library of Congress bears no responsibility for the accuracy, legality, or content of the external site or for that of subsequent links. Contact the external site for answers to questions regarding its content.

Self-Assessment Tools: The website provides access to generalized clinical (self-administered) risk assessment tools/tests.

These tools, most often aligned to key services offered by the provider organization (e.g. heart health, oral health), provide users with a basic understanding of their risk for developing certain health conditions. Provider organizations deploying self-assessment tools usually leverage the findings to spur users to share the findings with their doctor or other clinical professional. Websites offering self-administered assessment tools should include some type of disclaimer regarding the assessment. More specifically, the findings are for educational purposes only and not to diagnose or make treatment decisions.

3. Experiential

The third and final type of *Enlightening* health content provider organizations place on their website centers on the patient experience. For most patients, exposure to the uncertainty of healthcare interventions can trigger some degree of fear. In the face of fear, individuals respond by arming themselves to combat the perceived threat (the "fight" response) or remove themselves from the situation (the "flight" response). The intent of *experiential* information is to help the patient understand and/or prepare for their care by addressing the patient's rational and emotive self-preservation concerns. More specifically, *experiential* information intends to comfort patients by informing them of external protective resources and relating the health experiences of their peers.

Experiential enlightenment can be established and reinforced through the following:

Patient Advocacy Services: The website provides information on patient advocacy services (e.g. dealing with insurance or navigating the system).

Patient advocacy is an area of specialization in healthcare involving a third-party support for patients and caregivers. The patient advocate may be an individual or an organization, often, though not always, concerned with one specific group of disorders.

Patient Rights: The website provides some statement about the rights of patients.

The specific rights granted to patients will of course vary of jurisdiction, with some rights guaranteed by federal law and other commitments voluntarily offered by the provider organization. An important patient right addressed by most, if not all countries, is informed consent. This means that healthcare providers must give patients the information needed to decide whether to accept a prescribed treatment intervention.

Patient Stories: The website provides patient experience stories.

Pharmaceutical companies have long used carefully scripted actors or celebrities to be spokespeople for their products, and for good reason; patients tend to trust reviews and referrals that come from individuals who they perceive to be like themselves. Testimonials from real patients, with a positive outcome, can provide a reassuring example at a time when many people are anxious about their healthcare or that of a loved one. These stories, when highlighting the gentle care and concern delivered by the staff, can help reinforce the idea of the "high-touch" characteristics of the provider organization. As such, patient experience stories can be among the most effective and relatable tools for educating website visitors.

Summary

Concerns surrounding one's personal health can move a patient to seek reassurances from formal health institutions (albeit a physician or a provider organization's website) that their personal health needs and interests are not only shared by others but also a course of action exists to remedy their concerns. One way for individuals to satisfy their need for validation is to educate themselves on relevant health matters. To exploit these demands, provider organizations should leverage their website to include content assisting consumers and patients to associate their individual health interests and experiences with established knowledge and resources. Referred to as *Enlightening* in the HEWSi™ framework, the type of health information individuals seek of course varies by the specific issue. That said, Enlightening health web content arguably partitions into three categories:

1. Care environment
2. Clinical
3. Experiential

Discussion Questions

1. How does *Enlightening* support a provider organization's digital culture?
2. The *Enlightening* domain assumes patients are motivated to seek reassurances from recognized health professionals/institutions regarding their personal health needs and concerns, and that a provider organization's website is an acceptable "recognized" resource. Do you agree with this argument? Explain your answer.
3. Discuss the pros and cons of making self-assessment tools available on a provider organization's website.
4. A considerable amount of the discussion in this chapter was devoted to the topic of CAM. Given the historical tension between CAM and traditional medicine advocates, what advice would you have for a traditional medical provider organization considering the inclusion of CAM-related information on their website?
5. If you had to choose one of the RSS news feeds identified earlier in the chapter for consumers visiting a hospital's website, which one would you select? Explain why you selected this one.

Chapter 4

Aligning

The Challenge of Healthcare Marketing

The components of a health organization's website discussed up to this point have functioned to attract, inform, and retain website visitors. The information shared is highly static with website visitors largely assuming a passive role; they are receptors of information the provider organization shares. Unless the website purposes to be nothing more than an "electronic brochure" for the organization, websites should offer website visitors the opportunity to take some type of action to support the provider organization's efforts.

A website's facilitation of audience behavior is most evident when allowing for the purchase of products. Confirmation of a website's impact in converting visitors from browsers to buyers in these situations can be measured in "click-throughs" (the ratio of users who click on a specific link to the number of total users who view a page, email, or advertisement) and the volume of transactions handled via the website. While these impact measures make sense when dealing with retail-orientated websites, it is not immediately clear if these same measures apply to healthcare provider organizations. There are peculiarities associated with the marketing of provider organizations that challenge the utility of websites as a channel for influencing patient behavior.

The first challenge surrounds the type of the "thing" being marketed on the website. As a provider organization's core business involves the delivery of a "service" (as opposed to a consumable good), the marketing focus of the website should naturally be on the services offered. However, marketing a service is different from marketing a consumable. In fact, there are four issues distinguishing service marketing from consumable goods marketing that provider organizations must address in their website marketing efforts:

Intangibility: Patients/consumers are unable to view or experience the thing they are buying prior to purchasing it, because there is nothing (or at the very least very little) about the service that can be perceived by the physical senses.

Perishability: Services are delivered only in the moment they are produced. There is no need for inventory controls.

Inseparability: The production and consumption of the service deliverable happen simultaneously. There is no way to be able to separate the two. For example, patient care only happens when a nurse does something of value for a patient, albeit delivering medications or observing the patient in an Emergency Room bed.

Variability: The service industry relies on people to deliver the service in the moment. This human element means producers are unable to ensure a consistency in the final deliverable. This variability can vary across healthcare providers or even within the same provider organization. It can vary across time and across the point-of-care sites.

The second challenge surrounds the irrationality of the healthcare market. Below are seven "irrational" components of the healthcare marketplace digital media leaders from provider organizations should recognize:

Lack of consumer knowledge: Few healthcare consumers know the price or the particulars about the healthcare service they receive.

Lack of supply and demand: Under normal circumstances, there is a well-defined association between the demand for a service and the price for that service. This relationship does not necessarily exist in healthcare. In fact, there is little connection between the number of physicians (supply) and the prices paid for those services. In most cases, the billable rate is set by a third party (e.g. the government or insurance company), and not by what the consumer is willing to pay.

Consumption not based solely on economics: General economic principles do not apply to the consumption of health services. When a health issue arises, people need the service at that point in time. Running a sale on the price charged for a visit to the Emergency Room, for example, has no connection whatsoever to the consumer's behaviors.

Healthcare providers cannot refuse someone emergency services based on the individual's ability to pay: In the United States, as in most countries, a hospital Emergency Department cannot refuse to treat patients presenting with a health need (e.g. broken wrist) if they are unable to pay.

Acute healthcare providers (for the most part) cannot only provide profitable services: Hospital providers need to provide a wide range of services to include those services in which they lose money.

Lack of industry data: By history, healthcare has not done a very good job in collecting information about the healthcare consumer industry. While this is changing, marketers have a long history of applying their trade "in the dark".

Lack of substitutes: In the retail industry, the substitute for purchasing a T.V. (one form of entertainment/amusement) might be another form of entertainment/amusement, such as an iPad, or book. This concept does not hold in healthcare. If individuals need to be hospitalized, there are few good, equitable alternatives.

Given the complexity of the healthcare marketplace, provider organizations are understandably frustrated in trying to ascertain appropriate measures of a website's success. One measure digital media leaders in other industries use is the Call-to-Action (CTA) Click-Through Rate. CTAs are directives that drive website visitors to take some type of action (i.e. "download now", "view more", "add to cart", etc.). CTAs are a critical component of any website as they work to move website visitors from passive information receivers to active participants willing to associate themselves with the efforts of the host organization in some desired way, albeit as a purchaser of a consumable product or healthy behavior. To shepherd website visitors along their patient engagement journey, a provider organization's website should include some call to action designed to allow users to demonstrate their alignment with the provider organization. Thus, leading to the third domain of the Health Empowerment Web Strategy Index (HEWSi™) model: *Aligning.*

The "Aligning" Domain

Aligning in the HEWSi™ framework is defined as *website content designed to activate and channel website visitors to pursue some type of behavior supportive of the provider organization's efforts.* Under this rubric, the measure of success is for website visitors to "align" their behaviors with those expounded by the provider organization. As such, the flow of communication under the *Aligning* domain is necessarily bidirectional, with opportunities for website visitor-initiated communications more extensive than one would see under the *Orienting* or *Enlightening* domains.

Aligning functions in part to separate select market segments from the general population. Though presented to a broad audience on a provider organization's website, *Aligning* content purposes to stimulate defined visitor groups to take certain actions. For example, listing open nursing jobs at the provider organization is a call to action for a narrowly defined audience (registered nurses [RNs]) with the qualifications to answer the appeal. As the goal of *Aligning* is to activate website visitors, the content is understandably more personal to the visitor than *Orienting* or *Enlightening* content. Indeed, to stimulate targeted audiences to act, provider organizations are attempting to tap into some rational and/or emotional investment website visitors have of an issue addressed on the provider organization's website. Yet it is the channeling of the website visitor's emotional/rational invested behavior through a digital medium that helps cement *Aligning* as a significant step in establishing a provider organization's digital culture. The reliance on electronic tools through which targeted website visitors can align themselves with the provider organization sets an expectation for how patients can interact with the organization.

While the measure of success in *Aligning* is for the website visitor to take some type of action, not all actions are equally important. Some acts require a greater degree of personal investment than others. *Aligning* recognizes these variances and partitions the demonstrated support into two classes of alignment:

1. Resource Alignment
2. Intimacy

Given the progressive investment, the following will address the less inten-
sive type of *Aligning* (Resource Alignment) first, before addressing the more
personal *Aligning* manifestation, Intimacy.

1. Components of Resource Alignment

Resource Alignment refers to the use of one's financial resources (cash or
other assets that can be converted to cash) to express support for a provider
organization's efforts. While the personal value one assigns to money varies
by individual, *Resource Alignment* is ultimately a "commoditized" expression of support as cash is exchangeable and replaceable. As such, this type
of aligning is not as deeply personal an expression of support as the type of
expressions one might see in an intimate alignment scenario.

Resource Alignment can be established and reinforced through the following:

Membership Programs: The website offers visitors the ability to join a
provider-sponsored membership program.

Membership or loyalty programs, where consumers provide their
contact information in exchange for product discounts, are a common practice within the retail industry. Healthcare providers, especially
hospitals, have used this same tactic to build consumer loyalty to the
healthcare provider and to influence the health behaviors of its members through targeted health promotion campaigns.

The most popular hospital membership clubs tend to be geared
toward individuals aged 50 and over. While the early iterations of these
programs tended to be marketed as "senior programs", hospital marketers soon learned that the targeted age group avoids products or
services with a "senior" label. One way to overcome the challenge of
being perceived as a club for elderly individuals is to offer programs
tailored to both the young and old spectrums of the 50 plus demographic. For example, providing yoga classes in addition to estate planning workshops, or scheduling programs during lunch hours, evenings,
or on weekends to make it easier for working younger members of the
targeted market to attend. Giving the program a generic name such as
"Health Connection" also will broaden the club's appeal. More will be
discussed later in this chapter about the "selling" of desired social and
health behaviors.

Philanthropic—Information: The website provides visitors with information about donating to the organization.

Philanthropic—Portal: The website provides visitors an online portal by which to donate financially to the organization.

With ever-tightening margins from operations and investments, increasing debt, and healthcare reform, private philanthropy remains an attractive option to supplement capital expenditures, special projects, healthcare initiatives, or general operations. Indeed, philanthropy is a key lever in strengthening the organization to secure competitive advantage, spur growth, or sometimes keep the doors open. Yet philanthropic outreach efforts should not focus exclusively on the wealthy in one's community. The 2016 U.S. presidential campaign not only illustrated the need for donor diversification but also highlighted a growing trend in fundraising: the generation of significant cash from small donations (a.k.a. microdonors). Health systems can benefit from creating a bigger pool of microdonors who are able to give smaller amounts. Gifts of $25, $100, or $200 can add up to help provider organizations further their missions. Websites can be key to the success of microdonor fundraising efforts. Provider organizations targeting microdonors not only need to create a website experience around the issues donors care about but also provide visitors an online tool by which to financially express their support.

Products/Services: The website offers website visitors the ability to purchase items (e.g. purchase flowers, car seats, "swag") or services (e.g. care sitters) through an online store.

A retail presence on a healthcare provider's website is an opportunity many organization's overlook. The reality is that a certain segment of the market with whom the provider organizations interact has a desire to purchase items (e.g. flowers, balloons) that can cheer up patients or express gratitude to the staff caring for a loved one. If the provider organization does not address this demand, someone else will. Virtual gift shops provide visitors with a means by which to satisfy this desire.

2. *Components of Intimacy*

Intimacy in the HEWSi™ context reflects more personal forms of alignment than the expressions of support evidenced in *Resource Alignment*. *Intimacy* includes a wide swath of expressions, such as the sharing of personal experiences with the provider organization on social media (e.g. Facebook), to electronically submitting one's resume for a job at the provider organization. Though broad in scope, the common denominator in an intimate alignment is the high degree of personal investment required of individuals. Here, the expression of support for a provider organization's efforts is based on nonfinancial resources. As such, intimate aligning is much less subject to "commoditization" than resource aligning and certainly less replaceable.

Intimacy can be established and reinforced through the following:

External Social Media: The website offers visitors the ability to publicly share their experiences via popular social media tools (e.g. Facebook, Twitter).

Social media has become an increasingly important tool provider organizations must learn to manage. Healthcare professionals are painfully aware of patients who, in the name of being informed, heavily research their health and what conditions they think they have. Practitioners are no longer considered automatic authorities. They have had to defend themselves against Google searches and Facebook posts. Consumers increasingly rely on social media to help manage their health. Given the heavier use by younger people, this trend is likely to sharply increase over time. Things get more complicated when a growing percentage of consumers use what they see on social media to impact how they handle their health. This can result in health professionals having significant battles with their patients if the professionals' advice does not match the wisdom of the crowd.

This is not to suggest that public facing social media is bad. There are definitely pluses to social media, especially as a vehicle by which to reach and interact with targeted patient groups. Social media also allows organizations to interact with their patient population in real time on a more personal level. Patients engage with healthcare organizations on social media with the expectation that they will receive a friendly and helpful response. But to respond quickly and accurately, it's best to have responses predrafted to address common questions, comments, and concerns in the following areas:

Medical advice: While it is important not to provide a diagnosis over the Internet, it is critical to have multiple responses drafted for patients who are looking for medical advice. These types of pre-drafted responses present an opportunity for provider organizations to redirect patients to the appropriate doctor or service group within one's organization. An example of a solid response might be:

> Hi Jane, thank you for reaching out to us about your situation. Dr John Smith, medical director of our wound care center, is an expert in head wounds and would be the best person to help you. Please give him a call at 555-1234 to set up an appointment.

This response shows that your organization is helpful; it also highlights your doctor's expertise and drives a patient into your facility.

Bad service: Provider organizations should address complaints about bad service on social media promptly and respectfully. A quick and helpful response will show the patient (and all other patients who have seen the public complaint) that your organization cares about the patient experience and can provide prompt, high-quality service. For less common questions, or questions that require a customized response, make sure there is a plan in place. For example, if someone is experiencing technical difficulties with the website, the response matrix should outline the process for quickly getting in touch with the information technology team to identify the problem and draft a helpful response to the patient.

The world of social media marketing has changed significantly over the past decade or so. These changes are driven by trends in patient behavior and preferences, especially *Gen Z* and *millennial* markets. Reaching out to younger members of society means that healthcare marketers need to change their communication models and focus on what matters to the younger generation. Regardless of the size and specialty of the provider organization, social media has proven to be an effective medium. Social networks have a captive and thriving audience and provide endless opportunities for healthcare marketers to build meaningful relationships with their target audience.

Below are a few social media trends provider organizations should recognize as they leverage this tool in fostering patient alignment.

Increased Use of Video Content: Video content has grown exponentially in popularity over the last few years. Widely recognized as being one of the most engaging mediums, mobile video, to include live streaming, is emerging as an influential resource for generating patient interest in health services. An excellent way to utilize video is by creating and sharing short clips of patients or clinicians sharing personal stories about select services. Overall, having the ability to create relevant video content in multiple formats on a regular basis and strategically tied to supportive content (e.g. blogs) will be critical for web marketers in the future.

Increased Emphasis on User-Generated Content: Social networks present many exciting opportunities to use user-generated content into building healthy relationships with prospective and existing patients. To illustrate, providers can ask followers to submit reviews or share experiences of their interactions with the provider organization on social networks. Providers can then choose the best submissions and share them on the organization's website, giving credit to the followers who submitted them. This is not just a great way to get fresh content regularly but is also a proven strategy for engaging potential and existing patients. Chosen followers will be motivated and will be more likely to recommend the provider's services to their family and friends.

Using Chatbots and Messaging Apps to Improve Patient Services: Chatbots give provider organizations the opportunity to interact quickly with their target audience in a way that feels personal. Though healthcare organizations need to be extra mindful of privacy concerns in using these resources, chatbots and messaging apps can significantly enhance the quality of patient service.

The Increased Reliance on Influencer Marketing: Social media influencers have an incredible reach, often with followings in thousands or millions. Healthcare marketers can pay influencers as a way to communicate with their target audiences and to promote the organization's services and/or desired health behaviors.

The Decline of Organic Reach Marketing Efforts: An approach favored by many marketers has been to "blast" a marketing message to a wide array of newsfeeds with the hope that entities will pick up the content and resend through their medium. Also known as *spam marketing* (sending irrelevant or inappropriate marketing messages to a large number of internet recipients), this approach has been a low cost way for organizations to generate awareness and business. With increased numbers of businesses leveraging their presence on social networks to "spam" web visitors, aggressive efforts to combat *spamming* has reduced the effectiveness of this marketing tactic. As a result, healthcare marketers need to be more selective about what and where to post content. With many businesses increasingly disappearing from newsfeeds, healthcare marketers need to purposefully choose the networks where they post content and be willing to invest in paid ads and influencer strategies.

Ephemeral Content Can Activate Patients: Ephemeral content is short-lived content that appears for just 24 h and then disappears on its own. This type of content is immensely popular among younger audiences. Because information is lost within hours, audiences interested in organization's ephemeral content are forced to closely follow the content storyline and act fast when prompted.

Live Streaming: While live streaming has been around for a while now, its use has grown at an alarming rate the last few years. Live streaming is a nearly free way to drive traffic to an organization's social media site and generate revenue for the organization.

Internal Social Media: The website offers visitors the ability to share their experiences, concerns, and suggestions privately to the provider organization's leaders through an email or electronic form.

The emphasis on patient-centered care has increased calls for transparency of patient satisfaction data. These trends in healthcare make seeking and responding to patient feedback increasingly important components of risk management and patient safety programs. Patients have the right to file complaints and grievances with the organization when they are unsatisfied with the treatment received, and healthcare organizations should have processes in place for handling both in a timely manner. In addition, tracking and trending of patient complaints and grievances may call attention to systems or individual performance problems and suggest quality improvement opportunities. For example, patient complaints are associated with both clinical complications and increased risk of malpractice litigation.

In many jurisdictions, healthcare organizations must develop processes for addressing patient complaints and grievances in order to comply with federal regulations and accreditation standards, as well as to protect patients and reduce liability. Complaints stem from minor issues that can typically be resolved by staff present at the time the concern is voiced, while grievances are more serious and generally require investigation into allegations regarding the quality of patient care. Provider organizations should look at complaints and grievances as performance improvement opportunities.

To effectively manage and leverage these types of expressions, provider organizations should consider the following actions:

- Design a process to capture and address all complaints and grievances.
- Ensure the involvement of the organization's governing body or its designated grievance committee.
- Implement policies, procedures, and processes for investigation and resolution of patient complaints and grievances.
- Educate all physicians and staff on grievance processes.
- Train all staff to listen effectively and manage patient and family expectations.
- Use dedicated staff to solve small problems before they escalate.
- Employ a proactive approach to customer service.
- Empower frontline staff to act as the first line of defense against complaints.
- Track complaints, grievances, and patient satisfaction surveys and implement improvement initiatives to address trends identified.
- Verify that the grievance process is effective.

Talent Alignment—Employment: The website offers visitors a vehicle by which to search and apply for employment opportunities with the provider organization.

Talent alignment reflects a highly involved level of engagement with the provider organization. Here, the website visitor is encouraged to give off their time and skills in supporting the provider organization.

Note that the wording used in describing talent alignment is purposefully broad to encompass employed as well as volunteer positions.

The looming shortage of healthcare talent continues to plague hospitals, health systems, and medical groups, as the labor market grows ever tighter. Healthcare employers must remember that, with low unemployment rates and growing job opportunities, competition for healthcare providers and other in-demand skills is severe. If a healthcare provider organization is pursuing top performers, it's safe to assume these candidates are interviewing with other employers, as well. That is why creating a consistent, credible, and responsive candidate experience is so important. Consistency of information and credibility go hand in hand. From the first conversation a doctor or nurse has with a recruiter to third-party review sites and in-person interviews, ensuring as much consistency as possible is essential to maintaining credibility. This will not only help employers better compete for talent but will also help paint a clear picture of the culture and expectations of the job and attract better fit candidates.

To more effectively compete in a fierce labor market, many healthcare organizations have turned their attention to strengthening their employer brand, and for good reason. Organizations with strong employer brands are more likely to attract applicants. They are also less likely to lose new hires after the first 6 months and enjoy a decrease in cost per hire. To date, however, most employer-branding efforts have focused inward to improve organizational culture and employee engagement. What most healthcare employers have yet to master is how to harness these efforts externally—leveraging employees and recruiters as ambassadors to build their employer brand among passive and active job candidates.

Forward-thinking healthcare organizations are leveraging employer-branding strategies to target passive and active job seekers. They are going beyond broad-sweeping employee videos on a generalized career website to customize communications at the recruitment level, based on unique talent profiles. This type of precision recruiting requires content that is relevant, credible, and most important, specific to each candidate audience. If going this route, there are four employer-branding trends website designers should consider in order to support the healthcare organizations' ability to become more precise in their recruiting efforts:

Data-Driven Approach to Personalized Recruitment: Big data is playing a huge role not only in the delivery of clinical care but also in attracting the right employees to organizations to improve cultural fit and retention. With communication vehicles more targeted than ever, there is nothing to prevent job seekers from expecting to experience the same degree of personalization as they would on other websites. As a result, blanketed job alerts and template job descriptions are becoming outdated. And for good reason, searching for a career is a highly personal experience to a job seeker. To prevail, healthcare organizations must connect with job candidates on the cultural and lifestyle aspects of a job that matter most to them, not just the technical skill requirements. Ironically, data allows this level of personal connection. Big data gathered from real employees can help recruiters customize their recruiting strategy, based on the specific job, location, and candidate profile they are targeting.

The Growing Importance of Unique and Relevant Job Content: While personalization is a tremendous competitive advantage on the "human" side of recruiting, it is becoming a fundamental requirement on the technical side of recruiting. Search technologies, such as Google, that focus on the *relevance* and *uniqueness* of content are taking the lead in terms of organic search optimization. Algorithms, for example, that scour the Internet to serve up the best possible quality of information to meet a browser's needs, are measuring *relevance* in terms of shares with like users while *uniqueness* is being measured as content that does not appear anywhere else. As such, standard job description language and template job posts may hurt the search results for job posts in the future. Ongoing management and customization of job content that better targets and resonates with specific job candidates, and creates a more technically unique job description, has the competitive advantage in this new environment.

Measuring & Leveraging Employee Brand Advocacy as a Recruitment Asset: The advent of social media and online employer rating sources has forced employers to be more transparent than ever before. With the click of a mouse, today's job seekers can find out the "inside scoop" on what it is like to work at a certain facility. As a result, employee opinions are having a growing influence among job seekers, leading to an organization's workforce as one of its greatest recruitment assets. Leading healthcare employers are adjusting their recruitment strategies to leverage this important asset, beginning with getting a handle on the strength of an organization's employee brand advocacy. This can be captured by including a "promoter" like question on an organization's employee engagement survey (e.g. determining how many employees are likely to proactively refer an employer to friends and family, or how many are likely to share or post positive stories about their workplace). Equally important is understanding why employees are positive about their employer. The real reasons may vary widely from what senior management believes. Armed with this information, the goal is to internally promote an employer pro's while improving or at least explaining the restraints that govern the cons. Frequent communication and transparency will help align an employer's internal and external reputation and will increase the number of employee brand advocates.

Predictive Analytics Streamline Job Board Spend through Improved Accuracy: The proliferation of recruitment channels has resulted in employers spending thousands of dollars annually to post opportunities in all types of job boards. The plurality of channels has led employers to become more strategic in which job boards they use so that they spend less to get the same or better sourcing results. Predictive analytics tools are playing a huge role in helping employers to more efficiently leverage their job board expense by identifying the most effective time of year, or even time of day, that a particular job in a specific city should run on a certain job board, if at all. By eliminating the spend on nonperforming strategies, whether that means using a certain job board for janitors but not nurses or running a certain job post for 7 days instead of 30, employers are realizing significant savings while improving the number of candidates sourced.

Talent Alignment—Volunteers: The website offers visitors information on, and a vehicle by which to apply for, volunteer opportunities with the provider organization.

Volunteers play a valuable role in many hospitals. Through their time and energy, their assistance is manifest in several ways to include
– Responding to the needs of patients, patients' families, hospital staff, and visitors.
– Promoting the hospital and auxiliary as a caring organization.
– Enhancing community understanding of healthcare through educational programs and outreach activities.

– Maintaining ongoing sources of revenue to meet present and future requirements. (In some hospitals.)

People volunteer for many different reasons (e.g. a desire to help others; to fight boredom; wanting to feel needed, useful, and appreciated). Older adults tend to volunteer their time and talents more than any other demographic group, primarily because they tend to be out of the workforce and have time in their lives to give to causes. This growing aging population should be a part of a healthcare organization's volunteer recruitment strategy, and inclusive volunteer opportunities promoted via the organization's website should highlight benefits relevant to them.

To attract younger volunteers, many healthcare organizations are emphasizing how they offer ways to add purpose to people's lives through volunteering. In contrast to older generations that see charitable causes as separate from their everyday lives, younger generations tend to view the two as linked and want to live in ways that help them "give back". Purpose is a universal human need that is not just limited to younger generations like millennials, however. When organizations incorporate this mindset into their web strategy, it will be easier to connect with potential candidates.

Although some organizations in need of volunteers will still reach out to prospective volunteers via traditional methods (e.g. flyers on bulletin boards and radio interviews that mention how to get involved), an ever-growing number are leaning on social media as part of their marketing efforts. Social media marketing will be particularly helpful for video content. Videos posted to social media are especially useful for attracting young people to volunteer roles because younger generations watch videos regularly. Videos are especially effective in helping people empathize with conditions vulnerable population groups struggle with on a daily basis. By showcasing the struggles select groups face and then transitioning into examples of how volunteers are making gains in alleviating those burdens, organizations can create compelling stories by which to recruit volunteers.

Organizations should investigate ways to let volunteers assist from their homes. During Barack Obama's presidential campaigns, volunteers could sign up to join virtual phone banks. Volunteering online allows people to make a meaningful impact without encountering some of the common obstacles that can ultimately convince individuals to delay their intentions to get involved.

Targeted Behavioral Change: The website promotes specific desired health behaviors (e.g. smoking cessation, breastfeeding) and offers connections to programs/offerings designed to assist in adopting the promoted desired health behaviors.

There is a myriad of ways to positively impact social behaviors. Below are just a few examples:

Technology: Technological advances in developing automatic seatbelts that wrap around passengers when a vehicle door is closed has helped reduce motor vehicle fatalities by ensuring passengers are wearing a seatbelt.

Science: The development of nicotine patches has been used as an aid in smoking cessation programs by releasing nicotine into the body through a transdermal patch.

Infrastructures/Built Environments: The development and provision of water treatment plants and sanitation facilities have probably had the greatest impact on improving the health of societies in all of history.

Business Practices: The development of paperless hospitals has not only positively impacted the environment but also improved patient safety given the timely management of patient information.

The development and availability of these technologies and built environments have certainly helped to facilitate positive outcomes for society. Yet, in and of themselves, these offerings do not necessarily mean they will have a positive outcome for society. The intended audiences must use the solution for the benefits to be realized.

So how can organizations get people to adopt solutions designed to benefit society? Below are three common approaches for changing societal behaviors.

Show Me: Educate the intended audience on the dangers of their current behaviors and inform them about the benefits of the desired behaviors. The assumption in this approach is that an educated individual will use their reason to avoid a negative outcome and ultimately adopt the desired behavioral response.

> *Example*: Educate teens about the impact cigarette nicotine tar has on decreasing lung capacity.

Make Me: Compel people to adopt certain behaviors by passing laws or establishing policies that punish certain behaviors.

> *Example*: Impose an age requirement on the purchase of cigarettes and penalize retailers failing to require consumers to prove their age when purchasing cigarettes.

Help Me: Encourage people to want the desired behavioral response.

It's to this third approach that Social Marketing has been offered as a potential solution. Social marketing is an approach used to develop activities aimed at changing or maintaining people's behavior, for the benefit of individuals and society. At its very core, Social Marketing is about changing society for the good. A healthcare provider organization's website offers an ideal platform for promoting those behaviors the healthcare community at large deems significant to address (e.g. ensuring parents get their children immunized, breastfeeding).

Multiple definitions of social marketing exist, but of the various definitions floating out there, there is a general agreement that social marketing involves the following distinguishing features:

Behavioral Focus: Social Marketers are ultimately interested in motivating individuals to act in one of the four desired ways:
- *Accepting* a new behavior (e.g. start exercising)
- *Rejecting* a potentially undesirable behavior (e.g. start smoking)
- *Modifying* a current behavior (e.g. increasing their exercise regimen)
- *Abandoning* an old undesirable behavior (e.g. texting while driving)

Voluntary Behavioral Change: The underlying principle for Social Marketers is noncoercive motivation. Social Marketers want individuals to so believe in a "product" that they, on their own volition, act in a way that aligns with the social marketer's intentions. By appealing to an individual's freedom to choose versus compelling a person to act in a certain way because they are required to do so by law, organizations can still achieve desired outcomes without establishing what some might call a "nanny state". The added challenge is that there is a real possibility that the behavior advocated may not directly benefit the individual or may be a delayed benefit. For example, encouraging people to vote may not benefit the one who cast a ballot if their preferred candidate is not elected.

Audience Specific: Marketers, like Sociologists, recognize that society is comprised of diverse social groups, each having their own set of motivators and inhibitors. As such, a "one-size-fits-all" type of approach is not the most effective way to impact change in society. Social Marketers therefore spend a lot of time and effort to understand the different population segments in society, and then evaluate which of these groups the Social Marketer can best impact to affect a desired social change. Once selected, the Social Marketer will then develop a marketing mix profile for each market to be targeted, one designed to uniquely appeal to the targeted segment.

Society as the Primary Beneficiary: Unlike commercial marketing in which the intended outcome is designed to primarily benefit the owners of a company, Social Marketing is designed to benefit society. While there usually is a high degree of consensus around what is good for society, this is not universally true. The abortion issue is a prime example. Both sides of the debate use Social Marketing to affect social behaviors which they argue will ultimately benefit society.

Reliance upon Traditional Marketing: The Social Marketer's efforts are purposeful. As a rule, they don't work without a process by which to guide their efforts. Their systematic approach considers:

Customer Orientation. Efforts are designed to understand and leverage the motivators and inhibitors of select audiences (the consumer/patient).

Marketing Research: Research is a key component to understanding and leveraging the motivators and inhibitors influencing behaviors.

Target Markets: Knowing the various audiences out there, the Social Marketer realizes the efficiencies in focusing their efforts on select audiences. By leveraging the motivators and inhibitors of greatest importance for a select audience, Social Marketers stand a better chance of motivating a small group of people verses selling a generic solution to many people.

Objectives and Goals: As part of a systematic process, the Social Marketer clearly defines the measures of success for their efforts; measures that tie to some strategic objective.

4Ps of Marketing: To achieve these objectives and goals, Social Marketers develop tactics that take into consideration the 4Ps of marketing:

■ *Price*: What the cost to the individual/to society/to the healthcare provider organization is, if the desired behavior is not embraced?

■ *Place*: How to best reach those whose behaviors need to change? Where to make the solution?

■ *Product*: What exactly is the healthcare organization trying to "sell" to the customer?

■ *Promotion*: What messages are to be shared with the target market?

While Social Marketing relies on many of the processes associated with traditional marketing approaches, there are four major factors differentiating Social Marketing from other forms of marketing:

The Product Being Sold: This is perhaps the most distinguishing factor. In commercial sector marketing, the marketing process is used to sell *goods and services*, but in Social Marketing, the marketing process is used to sell a *desired behavior*.

The Primary Motivator: In commercial sector marketing, the primary motivator is to make *money*, whereas in Social Marketing, the primary motivator is *societal gain*. Because the motivations are different, the criteria by which audiences are selected for the marketing campaign are quite different. In commercial sector marketing, audiences are selected based on their ability to provide the greatest volume of profitable sales. In Social Marketing, audiences are selected for a myriad of reasons, to include the *prevalence of the social problem*, *ability to reach the audience*, and *readiness for change*. In both cases, marketers seek to gain the greatest returns on their investment (ROI).

The Competitive Set: In commercial sector marketing, the competitors are other organizations that offer similar goods and services or, at the very least, satisfy the consumer's needs. In Social Marketing, the competition is most often the current or preferred behavior of the target market and the perceived benefits associated with that behavior, including the status quo.

The Challenge: Social Marketing tends to be much more difficult to accomplish than commercial marketing. In commercial sector marketing, for example, the financial resources tend to be more bountiful, and the behavioral demands are less demanding. In Social Marketing, targeted audiences are asked to do some challenging behaviors:

- Give up an addictive behavior (stop smoking)
- Change a comfortable lifestyle (reduce thermostats)
- Resist peer pressure (be sexually abstinent)
- Go out of their way (take unused paint to a hazardous waste site)
- Be uncomfortable (give blood)
- Establish new habits (exercise 5 days a week)
- Spend more money (buy recycled paper)
- Be embarrassed (let their lawns go brown in the summer)
- Hear bad news (get a human immunodeficiency virus test)
- Risk relationships (take the keys from a drunk driver)
- Give up leisure time (volunteer)
- Reduce pleasure (take shorter showers)
- Give up looking good (wear sunscreen)
- Spend more time (flatten cardboard boxes before they are put in a recycling bin)
- Learn a new skill (compost food waste)
- Remember something (take your bags to the grocery store and reuse them)
- Risk retaliation (drive the speed limit)

Incorporating Social Marketing into an organization's website requires planning. The following outlines ten steps provider organizations can follow when creating a Social Marketing plan for their organization.

Step 1: Background, Purpose, and Focus

The first step is the most critical step as it guides efforts in subsequent steps. Social Marketers would be wise to spend the appropriate amount of time thinking through and clearly detailing their thoughts in addressing three basic questions:

What?
- Clearly describe the social problem being addressed and the groups it affects
- Identify the major causes of the problem
- Discuss previous efforts to address the problem

So What?
- Explain how the current problem negatively impacts society

Now What?
- Discuss how a social marketing effort could help the situation
- Identify what aspects of the problem your marketing plan attempt to address

Once these questions are addressed, Social Marketers are positioned to develop a marketing plan *purpose statement.* This statement is a sentence summarizing the goals of the marketing plan.

Step 2: Conduct a Situation Analysis

The next step is to determine the varied forces and factors of the *internal* and *external* environments that might impact the marketing planning effort. To aid in this step, Social Marketers should conduct a *SWOT Analysis* (SWOT being an abbreviation for *Strengths, Weaknesses, Opportunities,* and *Threats*). In a SWOT Analysis, Social Marketers first audit those forces and factors that are under their control, categorizing these variables as either *Strengths* of the organization to maximize or *Weaknesses* to diminish. Factors such as available resources, expertise, management support, and issue priority reflect an organization's internal environment because they are under the organization's control.

Social Marketers then audit those forces and factors that are external to their sphere of control and deemed to impact their marketing planning efforts in some form or fashion. The identified variables are categorized as either *Opportunities* for the organization to exploit or *Threats* the organization should be prepared to address. External forces such as culture, technology, demographics, and economic are typically not within the marketer's control but must be considered.

Step 3: Select Target Markets

The challenge of the third step is to select an audience in which the Social Marketer can "get their arms around". In this step, Social Marketers first look at their total market and then partition the population into like group-ings. Once completed, Social Marketers purposefully select the audience or audiences they will focus on for the remainder of the marketing plan. They also begin to "paint a picture" of the targeted market by gathering relevant information such as:

■ Their readiness to "buy"
■ Demographic makeup
■ Geographic location

One of the most effective ways to identify a segment of the population to focus on is to profile the market in terms of *Effectiveness* and *Efficiency*. *Effectiveness* in how impactful the organization can be in influencing the population, and *Efficiency* in how hard the organization would have to work to be effective.

Step 4: Select Objectives and Goals

In Step 4, the Social Marketer defines what they are intending to do and how they will determine whether the marketing efforts are a success. In establishing objectives for the social marketing plan, it is important to have at least one behavioral objective:

■ *Accepting* a new behavior (e.g. start exercising)
■ *Rejecting* a potentially undesirable behavior (e.g. start smoking)
■ *Modifying* a current behavior (e.g. increasing their exercise regimen)
■ *Abandoning* an old undesirable behavior (e.g. texting while driving)

In social marketing, the market's adoption or "buying" of one of these four behaviors is the ultimate end. If the marketing plan does not include a behavioral objective, then it's not a marketing plan. Sometimes it is appropriate for a marketing plan to include knowledge or belief objectives. A *knowledge objective* is appropriate when there is a piece of information that the Social Marketer wants the market to possess, and a *belief objective* is intended to impact the target market's feelings or attitudes. But in both cases, these are only included as secondary objectives because they support the primary objective which is to impact the market's behavior.

Step 5: Identify the Competition, Barriers, and Motivators

Step 5 is one of those steps that marketers tend to not spend enough time thinking through. But don't fall into this trap because this step is very important. In this step, the Social Marketer needs to deeply understand:

■ What the target market is either currently doing or prefers to be doing (this would be the *competition* to the Social Marketer)
■ What real and/or perceived *barriers* the market has to the desired behavior, and
■ What would *motivate* the market to "buy" the desired behavior

Step 6: Craft a Desired Position

This next step flows naturally from the previous step. Once market preferences and motivations are known, the Social Marketer can develop a *positioning statement* describing how the healthcare organization wants the target audience to see the desired behavior relative to competing behaviors. People often get a positioning statement confused with a tagline or slogan. Quite simply, a positioning statement is a statement that defines the benefit of the desired behavior to the target customer, and states how the desired behavior differs from the competition. In contrast, a tagline or slogan is a catchy advertising message about how the healthcare organization wants to be perceived by the target customer.

A well-crafted positioning statement should answer the following questions:

■ Who are you?
■ What is your business/industry?
■ Who is your target customer?
■ What are the needs of your target customer?
■ Who are your competitors?
■ What is the key benefit of your company over your competitors?
■ What is the unique benefit of your product/service, especially compared with your competitor's product/service?
■ Why should your target believe you can deliver the benefits?

Step 7: Develop a Strategic Marketing Mix

The Strategic Marketing Mix (also known as the "4Ps of Marketing") details the logistics of how the healthcare organization plans to influence the target market's behavior. The Marketing Mix is composed of four elements: *product, price, place,* and *promotion.* When developing the marketing mix, be sure to address the issues in the sequence presented here, starting with the *product* and ending with the *promotional* strategy. Decisions around the product, price, and placement of the desired behavior must be made *before* the promotional plan can be developed.

Product: There are three product levels to consider when developing the product strategy:
- *Core Product* consists of the benefits the target market values that they believe they will experience because of acting as desired.
- *Actual Product* describes the actual behavior.
- *Augmented Product* refers to any additional services or objects included in the offer or that will be promoted to the target audience.

The following table illustrates the product levels associated with select social marketing campaigns:

Core Product	Actual Product	Augmented Product
Reduce ill-health in newborn babies	Breastfeeding	Resource hotline, post-discharge instructions
Prevention of cancer	Conducting a monthly breast self-exam	Laminated instruction cards for placement on shower nozzles
Prevention of suicide	Know when to intervene and what to say	Gatekeeper training for teachers, counselors, and youth group leaders
Drowning prevention	Wear a life vest	Life vests available for loan at beaches
Saving someone's life	Becoming an organ donor	National Organ Donor Card

Price: Describes any program-related costs the target audience associates with adopting the desired behavior. These costs can be in the form of both monetary and nonmonetary costs. The objective and opportunity in using *price* as part of the marketing strategy is to develop and provide incentives that will increase the benefits or decrease the costs of the desired behavior.

Listed below are six tactics that Social Marketers employ to achieve this end. Notice how four of these tactics are targeted towards the desired behavior while two address the competing behavior.

Desired Behavior		Competing Behavior	
Monetary	Nonmonetary	Monetary	Nonmonetary
Increase benefits	Increase benefits		
Decrease costs	Decrease costs	Increase costs	Increase costs

Place: Place is frequently referred to as the *delivery system* of the campaign. In social marketing, place essentially describes *where* and *when* the target market will perform the desired behavior, acquire any campaign-related tangible objects, and/or receive any services.

Place is a significant concept for a Social Marketer to address in a marketing plan. The use of *place* can be the key to the marketing campaign's success or failure. Social Marketers need to be keenly aware of how the target audience evaluates the convenience of the offering relative to other exchanges in their lives. Digital health should play a significant role in the organization's placement strategy. The next chapter dealing with *Personalizing* explores several ways in which digital health can support the delivery of services in a social marketing campaign.

Examples of place strategies include:
- Making the location closer
- Extending hours of operation
- Being there at the point of decision making
- Making the location more appealing
- Overcoming psychological barriers associated with place
- Being more accessible than the competition
- Making access to the competition more difficult or unpleasant
- Being where your target audience shops
- Being where your target audience hangs out
- Working with existing distribution channels

Promotion: Promotion describes the communication strategy, to include
- *Key Messages*. What is to be communicated, including slogans and taglines. The key message ensures the target knows about the

decisions made regarding the product, price, and place, the benefits of acting as desired, and are inspired to act as desired.

– *Messengers.* Who is to deliver the message?
– *Communication Channels.* Media through which the target audiences are "touched".

Step 8: Monitor and Evaluate the Plan

Step 8 ensures that a rigorous program for monitoring and evaluating the marketing effort is established. In this step, the Social Marketer determines which program components should be monitored and/or evaluated, how to gather the information and how to analyze and report the data. The measures used by Social Marketers at this stage typically fall into one of the three categories:

■ *Output measures* which tend to focus on campaign activities.
■ *Outcome measures* which target market responses and changes in knowledge, belief, and behavior.
■ *Impact measures* which concentrate on contributions to the plan's purpose.

Step 9: Establish Budgets & Find Funding Sources

In this section of the marketing plan, the Social Marketer "crunches the numbers" on how much the campaign will cost to execute as well as identifying the marketing plan's funding sources. Up to this point, the marketing plan has been subject to change. Once the budget is finalized, the organization is ready to move forward with implementing the marketing plan (Step 10).

Step 10: Implementation Plan

The last step is to transform the strategies developed in the previous steps into specific actions. The implementation plan specifies who will do *what*, *when*, and for *how much*.

Summary

A healthcare organization's website can be a powerful resource in shepherding website visitors along their patient engagement journey.

This can be accomplished by offering content designed to activate and channel website visitors into pursuing some type of behavior supportive of the provider organization's efforts. Referred to as *Aligning* within the HEWSi™ framework, the measure of success under this rubric is for website visitors to take some action that aligns with the behaviors expounded by the provider organization. Recognizing that not all actions are equally important, the HEWSi™ *Aligning* framework differentiates behaviors based on the emotional investment required of the website visitor.

Resource Alignment, the use of one's financial resources to express support for a provider organization's efforts, reflects a "commoditized" expression of support. Providers can establish and reinforce *Resource Alignment* by offering website visitors opportunities to purchase products/ services and give to philanthropic causes. As cash is exchangeable and replaceable, this type of *Aligning* is not as deeply personal an expression of support as the type of expressions one might see in *Intimacy*, the other type of *Aligning* in the HEWSi™ framework. *Intimacy* in the HEWSi™ context reflects behaviors requiring a high degree of personal investment. The expression of support for a provider organization's efforts is based on nonfinancial resources. Organizations can channel *Aligning—Intimacy* behaviors on the organization's website through the following; Internal and External Social Media, the promotion of Volunteering and Employment opportunities, and Social Marketing campaigns.

Discussion Questions

1. How does *Aligning* support a provider organization's digital culture?
2. Search for a hospital membership program on the internet. Describe the benefits the organization offers members. How is this organization using digital health to support their program?
3. *Talent Alignment* is categorized under the *Intimacy* rubric and not *Resource Alignment*. Do you agree with this placement? Explain your answer.
4. Search the internet for examples of healthcare provider organizations incorporating videos as part of their social media presence. What are they promoting, and what is the "call to action"?
5. A considerable amount of the discussion in this chapter focused on the development of a social marketing plan. Search the internet for a health

behavioral issue promoted by a healthcare organization (e.g. wellness checks for newborns, smoking cessation classes). If you had developed the social marketing plan for the example selected, what measures would you include in the marketing plan (Step 8) to assess the role digital health was having on the program?

Chapter 5

Personalizing

Provider Websites as a Tool to Merge Provider and Care Consumer Data

One of the most impressive changes our society has witnessed in the last few decades is the growth of what many call the *Web Economy*. The *Web Economy* is a new way of doing business, whereby companies use information and technology as facilitators of communication, data transfer, and commercial transactions. Reflected in the business models of companies like Amazon, Uber, and Netflix, many organizations have succeeded in this new economy by leveraging information and technology to offer seamless, customer-centric digital experiences in industries once riddled with inefficiencies. The exponential spread of the web economy has raised expectation as to what service providers should be able to offer consumers regardless of the industry, to include healthcare.

Evidence of the web economy in the healthcare ecosystem abounds. An array of digital health tools, such as personal health records (PHRs), various mobile health (mHealth) applications (apps), as well as patient portals, have emerged with the sole purpose to help patients better participate in their own care. These tools have proliferated alongside the explosive growth of low-cost, stand-alone wearable devices collecting a myriad of patient-generated health data (PGHD), to include physical activity, weight, blood pressure, heart rate, temperature, and even blood glucose information. Healthcare provider organizations have sought to advance patient engagement by leveraging personal health information and data. By integrating this type of data into the organization's information systems, ensuring patients have ready access to this information and providing customized tools and individualized care plans, organizations are empowering patients to realize their optimal health and wellness goals. These efforts also work to foster digital cultures, where being digitally "known" by one's healthcare provider organization is a good thing.

The concept of being digitally "known" is a foundational idea of the fourth domain of the Health Empowerment Web Strategy Index (HEWSi™) model. Up to this point, the domains of the HEWSi™ model detailed in the previous chapters have been components of an organization's public facing website. As such, *Orienting*, *Enlightening*, and *Aligning* content and tools are nonspecific to website visitors and necessarily ambiguous in their application. This is not to imply that this information is of no value. To the contrary, the three previous domains function to exemplify to the general public, the organization's digital health capabilities. They signal to individuals seeking healthcare services, the type of digital culture one might expect if electing to use the organization's services. Advanced capabilities in three domains should arguably attract digitally sophisticated consumers and patients to the organization's services.

The "Personalizing" Domain

The fourth and final domain of the HEWSi™ model, *Personalizing*, differs in that the core content and tools in this domain transact exclusively in patient-specific information and data. The targeted audiences in this domain are not just website visitors, but known patients leveraging the provider's website. As defined here, *Personalizing* is *content and tools tailored to known individuals made available by a healthcare provider organization in a secure website setting designed to empower an individual patient and/or consumer in realizing their optimal health and wellness goals*. *Personalizing* represents the healthcare organization's most exacting efforts of leveraging their website as a means of facilitating a digital culture.

Three features of this definition bear mentioning. First, as previously cited, *Personalizing* content centrally involves a patient's personal information and data. It is limited exclusively to those patients and consumers with whom the organization has a "known" relationship. Second, given the sensitive nature of the information and data involved, *Personalizing* content and tools must be offered exclusively through a secure web sign-in (e.g. patient portal). Because *Personalizing* is designed to transact with specific known individuals, patients must make themselves known in order to access the content and tools. A password-protected secure environment, like a patient portal, is well suited for personalizing activities. Finally, the expressed intent of *Personalizing* is to enable known individuals to use personal health information and data in taking some type of action towards achieving an individual health and wellness goal. It is this individualized enabling function that can be used to differentiate the various manifestations of *Personalizing*.

Components of *Personalizing*

Of the domains discussed so far, *Personalizing* arguably reflects the broadest array of content and tools provider organizations offer users of their website. To harness the varied constituents of this domain into a coherent format, the content and tools under this domain can be collated into the following three components:

1. Empowering Access
2. Empowering Control
3. Optimizing Empowerment

1. Empowering Access

The first component of *Personalizing*, *Empowering Access*, involves the idea of *equipping*. To take some type of action that moves a person closer to a desired end state, individuals need to have access to resources that help propel them in an informed direction. As such, there are two resources through which *Personalizing* purposes to equip patients:

A. Information
B. Tools

A. Empowering Access to Information

Access to accurate information is a key ingredient to ensuring patients make informed decisions about their care. The following reflect varied types of information provider organizations can make available to patients in a secure environment.

Billing Information: Patients can view their bill.

The extent to which patients are responsible for expenses incurred during an encounter with a healthcare provider varies by country and health system. Patients in the United States, for example, bear a greater personal financial responsibility for services rendered than patients in most other countries. It follows then that the priority healthcare providers place on this aspect of personalizing varies. That said, most Western healthcare delivery systems charge patients for select services (e.g. having a phone in one's hospital room). As such, allowing patients the ability to view any charges they have incurred is not an issue limited to U.S. healthcare providers.

Clinical Information—Download: Patients can download their electronic health record (EHR) (e.g. lab results, medical images, medication, medical summaries).

Downloading one's EHR into human and machine-readable formats permits an individual to do "something" with the record (e.g. print as a hardcopy, prepare to transmit to another provider). The downloading ability expands the patient's access to the information in the EHR, beyond restricting access to the EHR to the patient portal.

Clinical Information—View: Patients can view their EHR (e.g. lab results, medical images, medication, medical summaries).

An EHR is an individual's official health document that is shared among multiple facilities and agencies. The role of EHRs is becoming increasing influential as more patient information becomes digital and larger numbers of consumers express a desire to have mobile access to their health records. EHRs include patient demographic information (cited previously) plus current and past clinical results/interventions, such as lab results and list of medications.

Clinical Trial Records: Patients can view records involving any clinical trials in which they participate.

While EHRs were designed to support payers, providers, and hospital systems, and not clinical research per say, the data in EHRs overlap with many of the types of data collected for clinical research.

This provides opportunities for data sharing and reuse without reentry or transcription, thus supporting open science and learning health systems. Yet the movement to use EHRs in clinical research has been slow. This movement can be accelerated by ensuring patients play an active role in delivering feedback on EHR usability, and be openly communicative about their experience as they contribute their information to trials. And as more patients have access to their EHR data, sponsors of clinical studies must earn the trust of patients to empower them to have access to their clinical trial records to accelerate research.

Discharge/Care Instructions: Patients can view their discharge/care instructions.

One of the most important parts of a patient's interaction with a healthcare provider is the discharge process. During this process, the patient's responsibility for managing their own care is acknowledged, and they are provided with specific instructions on how to care for themselves. Discharge instructions (also known as care instructions) provide patients with information on the expected progression of an illness or injury, treatment, and care use of medications and follow-up. This information is critical to a patient's outcome, yet it is also extremely overwhelming for a patient to comprehend and remember. Not to mention most patients are distracted during this process, as they are eager to get out of the hospital and get home. One way for healthcare providers to help patients better retain this information is to make the discharge/care instructions available via the patient portal so that patients can view at their convenience once they get home.

Diagnostic Images and Video: Patients can view images and video of diagnostic tests.

Allowing patients the ability to view diagnostic images and video is perhaps one of the more difficult and controversial issues provider organizations must address. Patients largely do not have the clinical understanding to interpret the images, which can lead to a host of problems (e.g. patient anxiety). Provider organizations electing to allow patients access to diagnostic images and tests should develop a communication strategy around when/how to interpret the images with patients before releasing the images.

EHR Integrated with Patient PHR: Provider organization integrates their EHR with a complete pan-organizational Personal Health Record (PHR) via one viewer or presentation method.

An integrated PHR essentially acts as a portal into a healthcare provider's EHR. It can offer patients as much access to data, scheduling resources and communication among members of the healthcare team as providers are willing to permit, and can also offer a convenient way for physicians and patients to create a shared patient record and formulate a shared treatment plan.

Immunizations (Public Health): Patients can view their immunization record from external national registries.

An immunization record is a comprehensive timeline of all vaccinations a patient has received. An EHR is set up to ensure that immunization records are complete and accurate. Immunization registries function to increase and sustain high vaccination coverage rates by consolidating vaccination records of children and adults from multiple providers into a common database. Allowing patients the ability to view their immunization history beyond the information entered into the provider's EHR can assist patients make informed choices regarding their health.

Patient Demographics: Patients can view their patient profile.

Patient demographics form the core of the data for any healthcare provider organization. They allow for the identification of a patient and his/her categorization into categories for the purpose of statistical analysis. That said, there is no universally accepted interpretation of what constitutes the term "demographics", as it specifically relates to patients. Minimalists would limit the term to *name, date of birth*, and *gender,* whereas a more expansive view might include *contact information* (address, phone), *ethnicity, primary care physician, insurance provider data, emergency contact information, allergies, major diagnoses*, and *major medical history.* The HL7 2.5.1 immunization implementation guide may perhaps provide some guidance here, as it lists 39 patient demographic data elements organizations can use to identify a unique patient.[1]

---

[1] www.himssinnovationcenter.org/immunization-integration-program/data-elements-for-patient-demographics.

B. Empowering Access to Tools

Arming information to patients is a positive first step to get them engaged in their care. But once informed, the next logical step is for the patient to take some type of informed action. The chasm between being informed and acting is bridged when patients initiate or activate some behavior. To help guide patients in following through on their informed decisions regarding their health, provider organizations can offer patients an array of tools. This leads to the second type of *personalizing* expression, empowering access to tools. The several different types of tools provider organizations may make available to patients in a secure environment can be collapsed into three general categories:

  i. Assessing/Tracking
 ii. Planning Tools
iii. Postencounter Tools

i. Assessing/Tracking

The first grouping of tools surrounds a patient's self-management activities. Self-management involves the healthcare tasks individuals must undertake to live well. These tasks include having the confidence to deal with the medical and emotional management of their conditions. Provider organizations can increase patients' skills and confidence in managing their health by offering digital tools supporting a patient's efforts to monitor and regularly assess their health progression.

Condition-Specific Self-Management Tools: Patients can access condition-specific tracking and reporting tools.

The array of tools capturing patient-generated health data (PGHD) is growing at an exponential rate. There are no shortages of tools and mobile device applications being developed allowing patients to track and monitor their progression related to specific health conditions (e.g. Pregnancy tracking, Fitness tracking, Healthy eating tracking, Chronic care self-management). The explosion in mobile healthcare (mHealth) stems from the conviction that increased patient engagement leads to better health, and that there is a lot of money to be made in these tools. Add to that, the low barriers for entry and the mHealth app marketplace can be characterized as the "wild west". But like any new frontier, the emergence of healthcare apps leaves a lot to be desired. There is virtually no data about what works and what does not in the use of mHealth apps. Providers and provider organizations need to be confident that the apps they endorse will do what they claim to do. Their reputations are ultimately tied to the performance of the tools they recommend to their patients.

Symptom Assessments: Patients can access clinically accepted relevant tools that allow them to report symptom outcomes.

A symptom is a sensation or perception of change related to health function experienced by an individual. Symptoms such as fatigue, pain, and nausea can be classified according to their severity and perceived impact on function. Symptoms add to the burden of having a chronic disease, such as cancer, and they affect virtually all aspects of life. Symptoms interfere with a person's mood, level of activity, and ability to relate to others. Symptoms are best understood when self-reported from patients at specific stages of specific disease types. With the increased emphasis on patient and family engagement in care and healthcare decision making, the importance of assessment using patient-reported outcomes (PROs) to achieve high-quality care is well recognized. A number of Symptom Assessment Tools are available for providers to make available to patients based on the patient's known specific needs.

ii. Planning Tools

The second grouping of tools supports the patient's health planning demands.

Advance Care Plan (ACP): Patients can access a tool that helps them detail their ACP.

ACP is the process of thinking about, discussing, and writing down one's wishes about the type of medical care and treatment one is willing to receive if they are unable to make their own decisions.

Care Comparisons: Patients can access a tool that allows them to objectively compare healthcare provider organizations.

Every day, consumers make choices about which care provider they or their families will use. Often, these decisions are based solely on the provider's general reputation, the experiences of friends, or where a physician has admitting privileges without the benefit of objective information by which to guide consumers. Organizations can help patients make informed choices about their future care plans by offering objective comparative information on area providers. There is an array of factors by which care comparisons can be based, to include quality outcomes, costs, and patient satisfaction. Of course, the critical factor for this tool to be valued by the end user is that the information presented is objective. Subjective comparisons present as self-serving and may actually be a detriment to the provider organization's efforts of establishing the organization as a trusted partner in the patient's digital health experience.

Preventive Services: Patients can access select preventive care planning tools.

A wide array of preventive services exists for all adults, as well as specific services for women and children. While not all preventive services can be leveraged using online technology, a growing number are, and can be offered by provider organizations as part of the digital culture.

Wellness Plan: Patients can access a tool that helps them develop a plan of action geared towards achieving personal wellness.

A wellness plan should consider all these varying dimensions of wellness: physical, mental, spiritual, emotional, intellectual, social, occupational, financial, and environmental.

iii. Postencounter Tools

The third and final grouping of tools support patients in addressing issues after the patient has had an encounter with the provider organization.

Care Experience Surveys: Patients can rate their care experience.

Patient satisfaction, or care experience, is an important and commonly used indicator for measuring the quality in health care. Patient satisfaction has been found to be associated with improved clinical outcomes, patient retention, and medical malpractice claims. It affects the timely, efficient, and patient-centered delivery of quality health care. Patient satisfaction is thus a proxy but a very effective indicator to measure the success of doctors and hospitals.

Care Reminders: Patients can receive alerts, reminders, and notifications about care plan activities.

Linked to the discharge/care plan information noted earlier, these scheduled notifications function to remind patients and their caregivers of daily care activities (e.g. log blood glucose number, medications), as well as scheduled follow-up appointments.

Community Health Programs: Patients can enroll in community-wide health improvement initiatives.

One of the specific activities providers can direct patients towards after an encounter is to be involved in a relevant community health initiative. Being in a community with others experiencing similar health challenges can help patients follow through on their discharge/care management instructions, especially when the motivation to continue wanes. Some of the more common initiatives involve targeted risk factors associated with leading causes of illness and death: Tobacco Use and Exposure, Physical Inactivity, Unhealthy Diet, High Cholesterol, High Blood Pressure, Diabetes, and Obesity. Provider organizations can help facilitate patient involvement in these initiatives, allowing patients to enroll in these programs from the provider website.

Online Patient Payments: Patients can pay online any charges they may have incurred in the course of their treatment.

A logical extension of allowing patients to view the monies owed for their treatment is to allow patients the opportunity to reimburse the provider organization via an online payment tool.

Service Requests—Appointments: Patients can schedule new/follow-up appointments with the provider organization.

With all the online tools now available to consumers, it only makes sense for healthcare organizations to empower patients to schedule appointments online too. Not only is it easy and convenient for them, it also saves staff time.

Service Requests—Prescription Refills: Patients can request prescriptions be refilled by the provider's pharmacy.

2. Empowering Control

The second component of *Personalizing* involves the idea of *patient data management responsibilities*. This component reflects an advanced digital culture norm, as the basis of this component is that patients have a responsibility for the integrity and utility of their health-related data. Here, organizations facilitate patient empowerment by granting patients administrative privileges to:

A. Medical records
B. The pan-organizational PHR

Central to this component of *personalizing* is the difference between an electronic medical/health record (EMR/EHR) and a PHR. EHRs and EMRs are often used interchangeably as both collect a host of medical, clinical, prescription-related, and patient communication information and often support tools to improve practitioner workflow. The big difference between these two electronic records is that EHRs allow data sharing across multiple, unrelated practices, while EMRs are in one location only. PHRs are different from EHRs and EMRs in that they are maintained by patients or authorized individuals rather than provider organizations. As such, they collect patient medical information, but may not necessarily track other practitioner-specific medical and diagnostic details. The reference to "pan-organizational PHR" above differs from a simple PHR in that "pan-organizational" qualifier indicates ALL of the patient's health records regardless of who maintains the record.

A. Administrative Privileges to Medical Records

Provider organizations can empower patients with medical record management responsibilities or control in the following ways.

Grant Access Permissions (EHR): Patients can designate whom (beyond the care team) can view their medical record.

Patients sometimes want others outside of the provider organization's care team, such as a family member or trusted advisor, help them in their medical decisions. To best inform the patient, these significant others could benefit by viewing the information contained within the patient's medical record. Provider organizations can facilitate the desired involvement of others by allowing patients to grant access to whomever they deem appropriate.

Record Correction Requests: Patients can request corrections to their medical record.

It is not unfathomable to believe that patient–provider misunderstandings and/or errors are sometimes entered into a patient's medical record. Allowing patients to view their medical record opens to the possibility that patients may notice inaccurate or incomplete entries. Once discovered, patients need a vehicle by which to easily request changes. Advanced digital health cultures facilitate patient-initiated medical record requests. Note too, in many jurisdictions, patients have a right to *request* an amendment to his/her medical record and physicians have a right to *determine* if the requested changes will be made.

Set Privacy Controls: Patients can restrict what information in the medical record, noncare team members can view.

An associated aspect of granting access permissions to individuals beyond the care team is to control the breadth and depth of information they can view.

Transmit Patient Record (electronically): Patients can initiate the electronic distribution of their patient record to whomever they desire.

Instead of patients depending on a provider organization to transmit their medical record to other providers, the empowered patient can initiate these transmissions themselves. This capability not only underscores the ownership patients have of their medical record but can be a valued feature when patients want to send their medical record to a provider or family member in an expedited manner.

B. Administrative Privileges to the Pan-Organizational PHR

Empowering patient data management control responsibilities can extend to the patient's cross-provider PHR, if the provider organization is involved in a pan-organizational PHR effort.

Grant Access Permissions (pan-org PHR): Patients can designate whom (beyond the various care teams) can view their PHR.

Similar to the administrative privilege associated with a singular EHR noted earlier, this component of personalizing involves the patient allowing access to their complete pan-organizational PHR.

3. Optimizing Empowerment

The third and final component of *Personalizing* involves the idea of *curation*. This component reflects the most advanced form of digital culture, as the focus here is on assembling, managing, and presenting digital health tools and resources that meet individual needs/preferences. Personalization is most impactful when patients receive individualized and automatically adjusted targets in relation to their high-risk status. Here, organizations facilitate patient empowerment through:

A. e-Consultations
B. PGHD services

A. e-Consultation

e-Consultation provides a way to deliver healthcare services online. With the help of e-consultation services, patients can gain access to medical expertise that otherwise would not be available to them. As an online delivery approach, e-consultation also provides a choice for patients to receive medical advice from online doctors immediately, no matter how far away from the provider they may be or how late in the day it is.

e-Visits: The provider organization allows patients to have asynchronous online medical consultations with their healthcare provider.

E-visits are asynchronous online medical consultations between healthcare providers and patients conducted through a secure environment such as a patient portal. E-visits are designed to use structured computerized medical histories to allow clinicians to care for a limited range of common nonemergency medical complaints which can be well managed without the need for a physical examination. E-visits are an alternative to traditional office visits and can lead to improved access to care, increased provider efficiency, good quality of care for specified conditions, increased patient and provider satisfaction, and decreased costs.

Online Health Professional: The provider organization offers patients the ability to chat online with a healthcare professional (e.g. Nurse, Social Worker) about health concerns.

An online health professional chat service functions exactly as a phone-based health professional helpline service. The difference being the medium through which the consultative service is delivered. Health professional helplines serve a multiplicity of purposes, with the primary benefit of deterring individuals of seeking high-cost healthcare services for matters that could be addressed via a low-cost medium.

Preferred Language: Patients can have e-consultations in their preferred language.

Perhaps the most fundamental step to establish in an e-consultation offering is the ability to communicate with patients in a language they understand. While most jurisdictions operate via a dominant language, this is not universally true. Nor does this hold true in areas of high migration/immigration. Many regions have known "pockets" where the generally accepted dominant language (e.g. English) is secondary to the preferred language of an ethnic group (e.g. Farsi). To ensure marginal patient populations are engaged in their care, it is essential providers be aware of the varied language groups in their service area and offer patients the ability for e-consultations in the most common languages used in the provider organization's service area.

Secure Messaging: The provider organization allows patients/providers the ability to exchange patient health information to one another via a secure and encrypted platform.

Given the widespread adoption of smartphones and similar mobile devices, one of the easiest and most effective ways to encourage patient engagement via digital technologies is through a secure messaging platform. Secure messaging apps can boost patient

engagement in several ways to include improving appointment atten-
dance, medication adherence, patient satisfaction, and supporting
healthy lifestyles.

Virtual Coaching: The provider organization offers patients virtual
coaching services.

Virtual health coaching provides the guidance and motivation some
patients want in order to put their health goals into action. Coaches
help their clients identify their health and wellness issues and collabo-
rate to develop strategies to overcome them. Regular check-ins allow
coaches to provide encouragement and advice, and to adapt strategies
as needed. The purpose of virtual health coaching is to engage patients
in ways that are convenient for them, using a variety of technology
platforms: laptops, tablets, smartphones, texting, email, and more. The
point is to make access to advanced-care professionals making clinical-
based decisions easy wherever and whenever.

B. PGHD Services

PGHDs are health-related data created, recorded, or gathered by or from
patients. PGHD can include health history, treatment history, biometric
data, symptoms, and lifestyle choices. PGHDs are distinct from data
generated in clinical settings and through encounters with providers in two
important ways. First, patients, not providers, are primarily responsible for
capturing or recording these data. Second, patients decide how to share
or distribute these data to healthcare providers and others. PGHD can
come from a multiplicity of data capture devices such as mHealth apps,
wearable devices, and other remote patient monitoring (RPM) systems.

RPM: The provider organization allows patients to submit and access
PGHD.

RPM is one type of telemedicine that has broad-reaching applications and impacts for many different types of healthcare specialties and
facilities. Advocates for RPM monitoring programs cite its potential to
help achieve the healthcare "triple aim", through improving patient outcomes, improving access to care, and making healthcare systems more
cost effective. Healthcare providers in the United States have been slow

to embrace RPM programs though because reimbursement has been limited, and there has been a general reluctance to put faith in mHealth devices used in the home, where generated health data might not be reliable enough for clinical care. This mind-set has been changing with the advent of clinical grade mHealth technologies and an increased willingness for payers to reimburse for these services.

Summary

Personalizing, content and tools tailored to known individuals to empower patients and/or consumers in realizing their optimal health and wellness goals, represents the most exacting efforts by healthcare organizations to leverage their website as a means of facilitating a digital culture. This domain of the HEWSi™ framework is fundamentally different from the other domains because of the individualized nature of the content/tools. *Personalizing* marks a significant step in a provider organization's digital fostering of patient engagement, as this domain is limited exclusively to patients and consumers with whom the organization has an established relationship, and all interactions take place within a private secured environment. The *Personalizing* domain is composed of three distinct components: empowering patient access to information and tools, empowering patient control over the management of data, and the optimization of empowerment.

Discussion Questions

1. How does *Personalizing* support a provider organization's digital culture?
2. How does having access to information foster patient engagement?
3. If you were responsible for developing a care comparison planning tool for a hospital, what type of information would you include to help patients to compare healthcare providers within a local market?
4. The discussion under the section Empowering Control differentiates the PHR from the EMR/EHR. What are the pros and cons of connecting the PHR with the EMR/EHR?
5. Search the internet for examples of healthcare provider organizations claiming to support PGHD. What type of data are they encouraging patients to submit and how does this support patient engagement?

Chapter 6

Form

Form Follows Function

The famous axiom "form follows function" can be traced back to the famed American architect Louis Sullivan (1856–1924). First penned in an essay titled "The Tall Office Building Artistically Considered",[1] the statement in context meant that the purpose of a building should be the starting point for its design. That the shape (form) of a building should primarily relate to its intended function or purpose requires the structure's function to be established first before considering its structural form. Since then, this statement has resonated with students of design beyond the field of architecture. It has been found to be as relevant to the field of biology as it is to website developers.

For the website team, "form follows function" means that the purpose of the website (its function) informs how the website is to be structured (its form). Indeed, the premise of the Health Empowerment Web Strategy Index (HEWSi™) model rests on the notion that a primary function of a healthcare provider's website is to foster patient engagement. The function of this mandate has been expressed progressively in the four domains established heretofore: *Orienting*, *Enlightening*, *Aligning*, and *Personalizing*. Once understood, the team can turn its attention to how the website design best support its defined purpose.

It should be noted upfront that the HEWSi™ framework has no particular interest in the creative aspects of websites. While arguably a part of the website "design" rubric, the HEWSi™ model does not care that an organization's website uses the "Zig-Zag" or "Full Screen Photo" layout. This is not to

---

[1] https://archive.org/details/tallofficebuildi00sull/page/n3.

diminish the value of website layouts or the creative components of website design. On the contrary, a visually appealing website layout is key to keeping patients on the provider organization's site and a valued way to differentiate the organization from other provider organizations. There are many excellent resources for website teams looking for guidance on the creative, visual aspects of website design. Rather, "form" in the HEWSi™ framework is limited to two main categories of structural issues:

1. Issues impacting *website users*
2. Issues guiding *content management*

The rest of this chapter explores the various aspects associated with these two categories.

1. Structural Issues Impacting Website Users

The first set of structural issues center on user experience. The subjects under this heading divide into the following four subcategories:

A. Accessibility
B. Confidentiality-Privacy (Privacy and Data Protection)
C. Target Audience
D. Usability

A. Accessibility

The Web is fundamentally designed to work for all people, whatever their hardware, software, language, location, or ability. This is especially true for websites like those representing healthcare provider organizations, targeting individuals with compromised physical abilities. Web accessibility means that a website is designed and developed so that people with disabilities can use them. The best way of ensuring accessibility is to comply as far as possible with the guidelines of the Web Accessibility Initiative (see www.w3.org/wai for details), which includes such things as using only structural/semantic elements in HTML code and separating out all design features into Cascading Style Sheet (CSS) files, as well as ensuring that alternate text is available for all graphical elements. That notwithstanding, this section addresses accessibility issues into the following six topics:

    i. Audio
   ii. Browser Compatibility
  iii. Compliance
  iv. Manual
   v. Software Compatibility
  vi. Visual

i. Audio

A popular way to share content on a website is to embed short videos. This time-based media oftentimes uses audio files to communicate its content to web visitors. To ensure accessibility for the hearing impaired, the web designer should consider the following.

Audio Controls: Website visitors can control the audio (e.g. pause, stop, change the volume) of any audio files used in the website independent of the audio controls of the device used to access the website.

Web content delivered via time-based media should allow web page visitors to control the audio file in terms of its execution (e.g. pause, stop, replay the audio) and volume independent of the overall volume level of the device used to access the website.

Auditory Descriptions: The website ensures auditory-only information is communicated via alternative mediums.

To ensure audio-only web content is accessible to hearing-impaired web visitors, the website should have a mechanism for presenting the same information in an accessible format (e.g. creating a document that tells the same story and presents the same information as the prerecorded audio-only content). In doing so, the document serves as a long description for the content and includes all of the important dialog as well as descriptions of background sounds, etc. that are part of the story.

ii. Browser Compatibility

A web browser (commonly referred to as a "browser") is a software application for accessing information on the internet. Browsers are significant issues for developers to consider, because the way a web page displays depends on the end user's web browser. Browser Compatibility refers to the way a web page looks in different web browsers.

Browser Compatibility: Website content can be interpreted reliably by a wide variety of popular browsers.

It is important to ensure that a website is compatible across different browsers because not all people use the same browser. Making sure a site is compatible with as many browsers as possible widens the website's reach. Web developers should build web pages so that they look consistent across a range of browsers. While there's no "magic bullet" that will make a site look great on all browsers, one thing developers should do to improve browser compatibility is to test web pages across a wide range of browsers.

iii. Compliance

Legislation protecting the rights of people with disabilities has gradually become more extensive and more relevant, reaching into all areas of day-to-day activities to ensure that barriers are eliminated. And while physical environment challenges often first come to mind when discussing accessibility concerns, it's certainly not the only challenge people with disabilities face. Organizations that have a public facing website are increasingly facing questions about their website's compliance with accessibility standards. A website is accessible when steps have been taken to ensure that there are no barriers preventing individuals with disabilities from using the website.

Disability Compliance: The website complies with applicable federal and local regulations governing website accessibility for individuals with disabilities.

Laws regulating website accessibility will vary by jurisdiction. In the United States, the law primarily governing accessibility is the Americans with Disabilities Act (ADA). Even though the ADA makes no mention of websites, Title III of the ADA has been interpreted by U.S. courts to apply to websites. For websites to be ADA compliant, they need to be accessible, where accessibility means that people with disabilities can access content, navigate your website successfully, engage with different elements, etc. The most universally accepted technical requirements for web accessibility is the Web Content Accessibility Guidelines (WCAG) 2.1. WCAG provides technical specifications to improve the accessibility of web content, websites, and web applications on desktop computers, laptops, tablets, and mobile devices for people with a wide range of disabilities—including auditory, cognitive, neurological, physical, speech, and visual disabilities. As U.S. courts and the Department of Justice (DOJ) have frequently referenced WCAG in decisions adjudicating accessibility, U.S. organizations would do well to ensure their website complies with the WCAG standards.

iv. Manual

Many websites leverage automated functionalities to enhance the users experience on a web page. Yet some of these inclusions are not appropriate for all web visitors and should allow for manual control.

Animation Control: Website users can manage the tempo (e.g. stop, adjust) of animated web content.

Animated interfaces can cause headaches, nausea, dizziness, and other health problems for many people. The most affected groups are people with vestibular disorders, epilepsy, and migraine sensitivities. However, anyone can experience similar issues if subjected to excessive motion on the screen for a longer period. Always provide more than one way for users to stop, pause, and restart animations.

Interactive Content: Website users can manage the tempo of web content in which user interaction is limited by time.

If the content of a web page involves user interaction, there should be no time restrictions on users. If content does include time restrictions, users should be allowed to postpone or suppress the time parameters, except when these imply an emergency. When an authenticated session expires, the user should be able to continue their activity without losing their data after being reidentified.

Keyboard Control: All functionalities of the website can be controlled using a keyboard.

A foundational factor for a website to be considered disability compliant is that any interaction and information from a website that can be accessed with a mouse must also be accessible with just a keyboard. The primary groups of people who tend to be dependent on a keyboard include the blind, low-vision users with a screen reader or screen magnifier and people with mobility disabilities that impair fine motor control, such as multiple sclerosis or Parkinson's disease. These groups may not be 100 percent dependent on the keyboard but is most likely to be their primary tool for interacting with their computer.

Keyboard Navigation: Website users can navigate through the entire website using a keyboard.

Navigating with a keyboard is very different than navigating with a mouse. When using a mouse, end users direct their actions by moving the mouse and following the visible cursor until it lands where desired. Users then engage the action wanted by clicking the mouse. Users are given a lot of cues about what they are doing because they can see the mouse cursor move, and the mouse cursor itself will change shape when it lands on something that's clickable. When navigating using a keyboard, actions are directed by the website. Navigating through a website with a keyboard uses the TAB key to move forward and the SHIFT + TAB combination to move backwards. These keys move you only between elements of the page that are focusable, such as links, input fields, and buttons. As an individual continues to navigate, they will jump between the focusable elements of the page in the order that they appear in the source code for the document which may not necessarily match the visual order of the page.

v. Software Tools

Website accessibility software helps businesses alter their websites and technology, so people with disabilities or specific needs can access a website. Website accessibility software often integrates with assistive physical tools to provide an inclusive web experience for the intended user. Website accessibility solutions complement integrated development environment software and other web development software by giving coders more tools to create accessible websites for end users.

Data Entry: Users are instructed how to correctly input data and correct a data entry error after a data entry error alert is issued.

Website visitors are sometimes requested to input certain data into a website form. The website should provide users the necessary information to assist in correctly entering data. Users should also be informed how to correct data entry errors. For website forms involving legal commitments or financial transactions, users should be offered the opportunity to review and edit their form before submitting.

Data Entry Errors: Users are alerted when an error occurs in the entry of data, identifying the wrong element and describing the error through a text.

When inputting data, users may incorrectly enter data. Website should alert users when errors occur, identify and explain the specific error, and provide help in correcting the error.

Definition Tool: The website provides a tool to define specific words, phrases, acronyms, and/or abbreviations.

Healthcare has a language that those within the industry use and understand but is foreign to outsiders. Healthcare websites targeted to the public should provide visitors with a tool to define words used on the website that are unusual or industry specific.

Discoverable Language: The default language of each web page can be detected by browser software programs.

Website users by and large prefer websites with content in their native language. If people don't understand the content of a website, they will move on to a site they can understand. This is a very real issue for healthcare organizations serving locales with immigrant populations. It is therefore important to give website visitors the option of a localized experience, and for that, you need translation. The problem is translating text from one language to another is not a simple process. Word-for-word translation does not usually work because there are nuances in language that get lost in translation. Such inaccuracies can significantly change the context of the message. One of the best solutions is to keep web page content for each language on separate URLs so that software programs can easily detect the desired language. Users should also consider cross-linking each language version of a page so that a French user, for example, who lands on the German version of a web page can get to the right language version with a single click.

Pronunciation Tool: The website provides a tool to help visitors pronounce specific words or phrases.

In a related way, some of the words used by healthcare providers reflect their Greek or Latin roots and are difficult to pronounce, especially for the novice. The website should provide a tool to assist users in the pronunciation of unusual words or phrases.

vi. Visual

Web developers tend to design and assess the web pages they create, using their own equipment's specifications. Using a fast computer and a state-of-the-art browser, they can turn their website efforts into a fabulous work of art. But not every person visiting a website is viewing it with the latest browser. Moreover, many sites neglect to address the challenges of visually impaired web surfers. When a website is built without regard to proper web design, they become inaccessible by people with vision loss who use access technology.

Contrast Ratio Color: The website uses a contrast ratio color of at least 4.5:1 for texts and images.

The Color Contrast Ratio is a property of a digital display system that considers the ratio of the luminance of the brightest color (white) to that of the darkest color (black) that the system can produce. To assist the visually challenged, organizations like WCAG recommend the contrast ratio color to be at least 4.5:1 exists between text (and images of text) and background behind the text.

Image Descriptions: The website provides text descriptions for all nontext content.

The website should provide textual descriptions of images used on the website in case the images do not show or are difficult to perceive. All nontext content (video/image) on the website has an alternative equivalent and descriptive that serves the same purpose.

Photosensitivity: The website avoids the use of visual media involving flashes or changes of luminosity that may cause damage or alterations to a viewer's health.

Individuals with Photosensitive Epilepsy (PSE) have a form of epilepsy in which seizures are triggered by visual stimuli such as flashing lights. Flashes or changes of luminosity on a website have the potential of harming these individuals. Given the potential harm that can occur from the use of such media, the website should not contain anything that flashes more than three times per second.

Subtitles: The website provides subtitles or audio descriptions for all audible content.

Information delivered on a website using audio files only excludes hearing-impaired individuals from receiving the same information. Therefore, any use of audile content should be accompanied by subtitles and audio descriptors.

Text to Speech (TTS): The website allows text to be read by TTS software programs.

TTS is a type of assistive technology that reads digital text aloud. It's sometimes called "read aloud" technology. With a click of a button or the touch of a finger, TTS can take words on a computer or other digital device and convert them into audio. As some people struggle with decoding and understanding printed words on a web page, TTS can help remove these barriers.

B. Confidentiality-Privacy (Privacy and Data Protection)

Confidentiality has to do with the privacy of information, including authorizations to view, share, and use it. Information with low confidentiality concerns may be considered "public" or otherwise not threatening if exposed beyond its intended audience. Information with high confidentiality concerns is considered secret and must be kept confidential to prevent identity theft, compromise of accounts and systems, legal or reputational damage, and other severe consequences.

Confidential Statement: The website provides clear information about its privacy and confidentiality policy.

The website should provide website visitors information on the organization's approach for handling private and confidential information.

Data Management: The website provides users information on how to manage personal information data concerns.

The website should inform users about their rights regarding identifiable patient data. The website establishes and shows the procedure by which the patient (the owner of the data) can access the data and, if necessary, modify or eliminate it. In the collection of personal data, the user has the option to reject the use of personal data for purposes other than those declared in the privacy policy.

User Protections: The website provides clear information about protections extended to users in the collection of data.

Data privacy laws vary by jurisdiction. The General Data Protection Regulation (GDPR) is a rule passed by the European Union in 2016, setting new rules for how companies manage and share personal data. In theory, GDPR only applies to EU citizens' data, but the global nature of the internet means that nearly every online service is affected, and the regulation has already resulted in significant changes for U.S. users as companies scramble to adapt. The United States isn't as highly legislated on a federal level as it is in other countries. Like with many issues, the federal government leaves a lot of details up to each state. Laws also differ depending on the industry, which results in a confusing mess of rules and regulations for U.S. website owners to navigate. The Federal Trade Commission (FTC) regulates business privacy laws. They don't require privacy policies per se, but they do prohibit deceptive practices. Some U.S. federal laws that touch on data privacy include the Health Insurance Portability and Accountability Act of 1996 (HIPPA), which deals with health-related information, and the Children's Online Privacy Protection Rule (COPPA), which applies to websites that collect data from children under the age of 13.

In general, data privacy statements should inform web users the purpose of any data collected, if the data is stored, and who is responsible for the oversight of the data. The website should also guarantee that the privacy of the user cannot be infringed upon without explicit informed consent, and that the organization will never disclose information that identifies the individual without his/her permission.

C. Target Audience

Healthcare provider organizations interact with a variety of audiences. The breadth of the population groups served requires representatives of the organization to ensure the intended audiences clearly understand which messages are direct towards them.

Audience Adaptation: The website curates its content for varied audiences.

Recognizing the varied audiences visiting a provider's website, visitors should have sections of the website designed specifically for their needs/interests. An innovative way to address this issue is to provide an opportunity for website visitors to identify themselves, and what they would like to do by visiting the organization's website.

Audience Identification: The website identifies to whom its contents are directed.

Provider websites interact with varied audiences each incented to visit the site because of their own particular needs/interests. Patients, for example, have very different expectations of the website than members of the media looking to investigate new developments in the organization, and vendor representatives try to uncover sale opportunities. While the website can be a singular platform to address the varied demands, patients need to be assured that the information they view on the website is designed to address their needs/interests.

D. Usability

Recognizing that the provider's website targets population groups with varied physical compromises, website usability can present a significant barrier to patient engagement efforts if not properly addressed. Website developers therefore need to pay special attention to a whole host of issues involving visibility, readability, navigation, etc. This section groups usability issues into the following five topics:

   i. Health Literacy
  ii. Labels

iii. Legibility and Visual Design
iv. Navigation
v. Organization of Content

i. Health Literacy

Literacy has traditionally been defined to mean the ability to read and write. The key to literacy is reading development, which begins with the ability to understand spoken words and progresses through to the decoding of written words and culminating in the deep understanding of text. Health literacy, on the other hand, concerns the degree to which an individual has the capacity to obtain, communicate, process, and understand basic health information and services to make appropriate health decisions. In addition to basic literacy skills, health literacy requires knowledge of health topics. People with limited health literacy often lack knowledge or have misinformation about the body as well as the nature and causes of disease. Without this knowledge, they may not understand the relationship between lifestyle factors such as diet and exercise and various health outcomes.

Acronym Definition: Acronyms and abbreviations used in website are defined in their first appearance on each web page.

Sometimes, website content will need to refer to healthcare acronyms and abbreviations. In these situations, in the first appearance of their use on each page of the website, the words should be written out with the short form placed in parentheses immediately after. This way, it's clear to the readers exactly what the letters mean.

Acronym Use: Website content avoids/limits the use of acronyms and abbreviations.

Healthcare is notorious for the use of acronyms and abbreviations (also known as initialisms). They are most often formed from the lead letters of words relating to medications, organizations, procedures, and diagnoses. Healthcare organizations should use these writing techniques sparingly, as their use can impact the safety of patients in hospitals owing to ambiguity and legibility.

Medical Terms: Medical terms used in the website are defined.

Healthcare organizations and providers often use terms that are unique to the medical industry. Those unacquainted with the medical terms will be challenged to fully comprehend what is being communicated. If the website uses medical terms, the terms should be defined in a way that is easy for a lay person to have a basic understanding of its meaning.

Multilingual: Website visitors can view website content in other languages.

Having a multilingual website may not be appropriate for every healthcare provider organization. This obviously depends on the community demographics. But the changing demographics in many parts of the world suggest unilingual provider websites will be the exception rather than the norm. Offering web content in different languages not only assists individuals from minority cultures find, obtain, and understand the needed information regarding their care, but signals the organization's desire to engage all members of the community it serves. While exceptionally useful, information in more than one language can add complexity to a healthcare provider organization's website.

Readability: Website content uses words that are simple and understandable by the targeted audience(s).

Readability is important to everyone who is producing content. Good writers wrestle to find the perfect level for comprehension and understanding. Free online tools (e.g. Readability-score.com and Readable.com) are available to allow content creators to check the readability level of website content.

Textual Brevity: Website content avoids using more words than necessary.

The average website visitor is not patient. They want their answers quickly and then they want to be on their way. For this reason, people tend to avoid "wordy" websites. To reduce wordiness, remove needless words and phrases.

ii. Labels

The labeling of content sections on web pages purposes to achieve two major ends. First, it helps partition web content into logical sections. Second, and more importantly, it helps website visitors in navigating a web page.

Titles and Headers: Web pages use titles and headers to help organize website content.

Headings are signposts that guide readers through web content. Because people tend to skim web pages to find the information they want, the titles and headers are valued parts of a web page. They should clearly and succinctly indicate what a section or paragraph is about.

iii. Legibility and Visual Design

Legibility is perhaps the most foundational issue included under the *usability* rubric. The usability issues here concern whether people are able to see, distinguish, and recognize the characters and words on the website.

Font Size: Users can adjust web page font sizes by using browser tools.

The ability to modify a website's font size to make it readable is a significant issue for many individuals with vision challenges. This is especially true for older individuals. While experienced web users will most likely know how to increase or decrease a web page's default font size (e.g. hold down the Ctrl key and move the mouse wheel up or down), this may not be true for every visitor to the website. Website designers should assist visitors in adjusting the size of web page fonts either by providing a tool on the web page (e.g. a scale bar that can be adjusted by a mouse and the plus/minus keys of a keyboard) or by instructing how to adjust the font size using embedded browser functions.

Font Style: The font style used makes text visible, distinguishable, and recognizable.

The style of font selected for the website is critical to the web visitor's ability to comprehend font characters. The font style selected needs to be one that is familiar to a broad audience. Many younger people nowadays, for example, are unaccustomed to the cursive writing style.

Printable: Website content can be printed without losing legibility.

On occasion, website visitors may want a paper copy of content they read on the provider's website. Web designers should support these demands by ensuring that the layout of the web pages allows for contents to be printed without losing legibility (e.g. the website uses CSS style sheets to differentiate between the structure of content and presentation). In the event that this is not possible, providers should offer a link to a printable version of the same content.

iv. Navigation

The ability of web users to navigate about the website has a bigger impact on the success or failure of a website than almost any other factor. The ease of navigating is fundamental to progressing website visitors from newbies to repeat users.

Breadcrumb Navigation: A graphical navigational aid allowing users to keep track and maintain awareness of their location in the website is clearly visible and accessible on all pages of the site.

A "breadcrumb" (or "breadcrumb trail") is a type of secondary navigation scheme that reveals the user's location in a website. The term comes from the Hansel and Gretel fairy tale in which two title children dropped breadcrumbs in order to form a trail back to their home. Just like in the tale, breadcrumbs on websites help users trace the path back to their original landing point. On websites that have many pages, breadcrumb navigation can greatly enhance the way users find their way around. In terms of usability, breadcrumbs reduce the number of actions a website visitor needs to take in order to get to a higher-level page, and they improve the findability of website sections and pages. They are also an effective visual aid that indicates the location of the user within the website's hierarchy, making it a great source of contextual information for landing pages.

External Link Alert: Hyperlinks to content/web pages outside the current website environment alert website visitors that visitors are being redirected to external materials.

In cases where hyperlinks direct web visitors to external content, the website should warn visitors that external content will be accessed, and that the user's navigation experience is subject to change (e.g. a new window will open).

Identifiable Links: Web page hyperlinks are easily identifiable.

Website designers embed hyperlinks in web pages, so visitors can easily move to and/or download content of interest to the web visitor. To maximize this feature, designers need to ensure that the visual presentation of links is uniformly recognizable and distinguishable from the rest of the web content.

Primary Menu: The main navigation menu is clearly visible and accessible on all pages of the site.

The Primary navigation menu reflects the content most website users are interested in. To ensure website users can easily navigate back to core starting points of the website, the primary menu should appear prominently on the website and be visible from all the pages that make up the site.

Search Engine: An internal search engine is accessible from all pages of the site.

Websites designed to support patient engagement tend to be content-heavy sites with many web pages. To help visitors quickly find the information they seek, organizations should make internal search engines available. To aid website visitors in using the search tool, the tool should be placed at the top of each web page's header or sidebar. Also, the tool should be clearly marked as a search tool.

Secondary Menu: If offered, a secondary navigation system (e.g. site map, table of contents, keyword indexes) is clearly visible and accessible on all pages of the site.

As a website grows in complexity, organizations oftentimes find that content doesn't always fit in one large menu, no matter how organized it may be. Secondary menus are for content that is of secondary interest to the user. Any content that does not serve the primary goal of the website but that users might still want would go here. For websites, the links might include FAQs or a help page. If a secondary menu is needed, then the challenge web designers often face is to identify which content belongs to the primary menu and which one belongs to a secondary menu.

Understandable Links: The purpose of an embedded web page hyperlink is clearly explained.

As healthcare organizations interact with patients reflecting a wide array of web skills and competencies, it is not unrealistic to believe that some web visitors will not know what hyperlinks do. To help visitors benefit from embedded hyperlinks, web designers should provide some explanation regarding the purpose of the hyperlink. This can be accomplished by including text immediately next to the hyperlink (e.g. *Click here* for directions to our north campus) or by using a hover box (a dialog box that opens when the user moves or hovers a mouse pointer over a trigger area).

v. Organization of Content

The content of a website is paramount to the site's success. It is after all ultimately what website visitors want when going to a website. High-quality content will increase the site's likelihood of converting visitors. But beyond providing high-quality content, a site also needs to organize that content in a way that makes it easy for visitors to use. Users should feel comfortable when they visit a website. They should feel that the site is designed, arranged, and filled with logical information that they know how to get to.

Continuity: The website presents a consistent design throughout the entire website.

Consistency is a golden rule in design. When website elements are consistent, users have a much more positive experience with the website are more likely to return. Web elements are the building blocks essential for a website. Patterns include header, footer, sidebar, and navigation bar. Web elements are the core framework of a website and should be kept in the same place to ensure a consistent user experience.

Logical Flow: Content is presented in a logically progressive and easily understandable manner.

Websites dealing with healthcare content transact with information that can be complex and targeted to a highly charged audience (e.g. patients grappling with a new diagnosis). It is essential that the flow of website content be presented in a logical, understandable manner to the user, according to some anchoring principle (e.g. theme, target audience). Each web page created should adhere to the same anchoring principle, in order to give website visitors the information they need in a way that makes sense to them. Most landing pages feature a headline, which should capture visitors' attention with a simple persona-driven value proposition, and a subheader, which should support or expand on that proposition in some way. As user scrolls down the page, subheaders and content should get more specific. A logical statement-and-explanation, macro-to-micro content structure on a web page helps usher readers down the page and streamlines comprehension.

Succinct: Web pages do not overload website visitors with excessive amount of content.

Content developers passionate and knowledgeable about a specific issue can easily get carried away with web copy. But writing web content is an exercise in selectivity and restraint. In a world full of distractions and saturated with competing interests, brevity is king. If website content is too complex, too wordy, or sprinkled with too much insider jargon, web visitors will quickly leave to read something else. This is especially true given that about half of web traffic is mobile. Target audiences don't want to try to find the info they're looking for in the middle of a wall of text on a palm-sized screen. When in doubt, stick with digestible chunks of straightforward language that's familiar to the intended audience.

2. Structural Issues Impacting Content Management

The second set of structural issues center on the management of web content. The subjects under this heading divide into the following four subcategories:

A. Content Credibility

B. eCommerce

C. Editorial Policy

D. Transparency and Honesty

A. Content Credibility

It is well recognized that the internet is full of a lot of bad information. Web surfers seeking health information have an elevated concern in ensuring the information they view is credible, given the impact the prescribed information may have on the health of individuals. To reinforce the trust bonds between website visitor and the healthcare organization, it is important for healthcare organizations to inform its target audiences regarding the veracity of the information on its website.

Accessing Content Authors/Owners: The website facilitates target audience access to those responsible for the website's content.

Website visitors occasionally have questions and/or concerns about specific content on a website and would like the opportunity to access those responsible for the content creation and/or publication. The website should therefore offer a means by which website visitors can exchange information with those responsible for the website's content, such as an email address, social media address, telephone, or mailing address.

Content Criteria: The website describes the selection criteria used when referencing external information sources.

It is not unusual for websites to cite external information sources. In such cases, website visitors should be informed as to why the information source was selected. This transparency affords the website visitor the opportunity to adjudicate the quality of the information presented and embrace the information as their own.

Content Datedness: The website identifies the date of the last revision made to each web page.

Website visitors expect the content they are accessing is current. Websites should therefore cite the publication/revision date of each web page.

Content Sources: The website identifies the information sources used to populate the website's content.

Website visitors should be informed about the various content information sources used by the healthcare organization. The referenced sources may include several potential sources to include the organization's staff, governmental agencies, or academic publications.

Identification of Content Authors/Owners: The website identifies those responsible for website content.

The website should identify the authors, editors, and/or persons responsible for the contents of the website.

B. eCommerce

eCommerce, also known as electronic commerce or internet commerce, refers to the buying and selling of goods or services using the internet, and the transfer of money and data to execute these transactions. As many healthcare organizations leverage their websites to facilitate these types of transactions, organizations should clearly articulate their policies related to the provision of electronic services on the website.

eCommerce: The website details the terms and conditions regarding the buying and selling of goods or services on the organization's website.

Purchasing goods or services via a website requires individuals to share an incredible amount of personal information. The information collected is highly valuable to and aggressively sought by companies for marketing purposes. As such, web visitors need to have a clear understanding of how the healthcare organization handles the personal information required for a transaction to be completed.

C. Editorial Policy

The editorial policy details the set of procedures used to select and publish website content. In doing so, the website owners provide website users with the information they need in order to make their own judgments about the veracity of the information included on the website.

Advertising: The website describes its advertising policy.

Advertising on a website provides a robust way for marketers to access very specific target audiences. The challenge with advertising on a website assumed to provide objective information is that it challenges the idea of the content's neutrality. Whether or not a healthcare organization uses their website for advertising purposes, the website should include a statement on how the website distinguishes between editorial content and advertising. If digital ads are used, the "Advertisement" should be clearly displayed.

Limitations: The website describes the limitations of the information provided on the website.

The website should include a statement noting that the information provided on the website is not intended to replace the relationship that exists between a patient and his/her healthcare professional, and that the misuse of the information on the website by nonhealthcare personnel could entail risks to the health of a patient.

Restrictions: The website provides information about the conditions or general restrictions on the use of the information on the website.

The website should include a statement noting the restrictions and conditions of use of the documents and information that are made available on the website. If the content involves licensed material, the website provides an external link to the entity or institution whose license, if any, protects the information or documents cited.

Support: The website declares its level of commitment to answer inquiries posed by users.

The website should offer a means by which website visitors can ask questions about the website's content, and the organization's commitment to responding to these inquiries.

Veracity: The website declares the healthcare organization's level of support regarding the veracity of the information provided on the website.

Visitors to a website should be informed to the extent to which the host healthcare organization stands behind the content of the information provided on the website.

D. Transparency and Honesty

Website users should be offered some basic assurances regarding the intentions of the healthcare organization hosting the website.

Financing and Sponsorship: The website provides information about its funding as well as potential conflicts of interest of those with responsibility over the website's content.

Most healthcare organizations are the sole financiers of their organization's website. Yet there are occasions when external organizations want to sponsor a healthcare organization's website in order to gain visibility with select audiences. As such, website visitors should be informed as to the various entities having a financial stake in the information provided on a healthcare organization's website. The users should also be informed of any potential conflict of interest that may exist in having external sponsors, such as a pharmaceutical company, exert some type of (real or perceived) influence over the website's content.

Purpose and Objectives: The website describes its purpose and objectives.

Often assumed, healthcare organizations should provide users with a clear statement regarding the purpose and objectives of the site.

Summary

The famous axiom "form follows function" is as relevant to website developers as it is to biologists or architects. For organizations developing a website, "form follows function" means that the purpose of the website (its function) informs how the website is to be structured (its form). Having established that a primary function of a healthcare provider's website is to foster patient engagement (as manifested in the progressive domains of the HEWSi™ model), web developers can then shift their attention to the "form" needed to support the HEWSi™ framework.

The supportive structure (form) of a website can be an expansive topic for web developers to consider. This is especially true given that the creative design components of a website are considered part of a website's form. And indeed, there are a multiplicity of excellent resources available to provide website teams guidance on the creative, visual aspects of website design. Yet, the HEWSi™ framework does not address the creative aspects of a web design. The framework is flexible enough to work with most creative web presentations. Rather, "form" in the HEWSi™ framework is limited to two main categories of structural issues: issues impacting *website users* and issues guiding *content management*. Issues impacting website users include topics such as Accessibility, Usability, Targeted Audiences (Audience Identification and Adaptation), and Confidentiality-Privacy. Issues guiding *content management*, on the other hand, concern Content Credibility, eCommerce, Editorial Policy, and Transparency and Honesty.

Discussion Questions

1. Why is it important to consider a website's "form"?
2. Select a healthcare provider organization and assess the Accessibility of its website. Describe what you found.
3. Select a healthcare provider organization and assess the Content Credibility of its website. Describe what you found.

Chapter 7

From Empowerment to Activation to Engagement

No Field of Dreams

Engaging patients continues to be a key initiative for healthcare providers to reform health care. Organizations throughout the world are aggressively chasing efforts to encourage patients to be more involved in their care. And for good reason, there is a growing body of evidence showing that patients who are more engaged in their care have better health outcomes and care experiences. It is therefore in a healthcare provider's (and the patients they serve) best interest to leverage their organization's resources, including their website, for patient engagement purposes.

Yet there are no easy answers on exactly how to increase engagement with patients beyond addressing their immediate healthcare needs. Building a "Field of Dreams" website to facilitate patient engagement does not necessarily mean patients will come and use it. What then can healthcare provider organizations do to move patients to be engaged in their care?

Empowerment vs. Activation vs. Engagement

To address this question, it is best to begin by distinguishing the terms "empowerment", "activation", and "engagement". Often used interchangeably, these terms have distinctive meanings, and are central to answering the question at hand.

Patient Empowerment: A multidimensional process that helps people gain control over their own lives and increases their capacity to act on issues that they themselves define as important.

A healthcare organization's website is a tool of empowerment in that it provides patients with the digital health resources to facilitate their increased involvement in and ownership of the healthcare process. The Health Empowerment Web Strategy Index (HEWSi™) model, as presented in the previous chapters, detail the various resources provider organizations could include on their website in order to empower the patients they serve.

Patient Activation: A measurable behavior reflecting a patient's willingness and ability to take independent actions to manage their health and care.

To be "activated", patients understand their role in the care process as well as having the knowledge, skill, and confidence to manage their health and health care. Digital health activation can be measured by singular patient activities such as registering an account on a hospital's patient portal, exploring a health application, or getting started on a health app task. Patient Activation is a transitory state as it represents the patient's initiation in embracing their empowerment.

Patient Engagement: A measurable behavior reflecting the patient's sustained activation and expansion of their empowerment as a patient.

Digital health engagement can be measured by the frequency patients log onto their patient portal, their completion of health app tasks, their feedback/suggestions surrounding hospital website features, etc. Much of the focus in the healthcare industry has been on Patient Engagement because health improvement is not achieved through a "one and done" approach. It requires sustained activation, which is what Patient Engagement denotes. It should also be noted that patients can become unengaged in their care and need to be reactivated.

Based on these definitions, the challenge healthcare organizations face with their websites is really twofold:

1. How to get patients activated in using the website and tools?
2. How to sustain patient use of the website and tools?

1. Strategies for Activating Patients

The first challenge healthcare organizations face with their website is to activate patients. For digital health Patient Activation to occur, organizations must know the specific patient being activated. Recognizing the progressive interactive relationship between patient and provider organization built into the HEWSi™ model, Patient Activation management and measurement efforts begin when patients are required to reveal their identity to the provider organization in order to access the available resources. Examples of Patient Activation behaviors include the following:

1. Downloading material about a specific health condition
2. Registering an account to access the organization's patient portal
3. Uploading personal health data into a health app

Though not exhaustive, below are a few activities organizations should consider as they look to stimulate patient activation.

A. Use Analytics to Determine Target Audiences

Not all patients are equal. In an era where healthcare providers are looking to have the biggest impact on the populations they serve, some patients present a higher priority for healthcare organizations to activate for any number of reasons (e.g. access to the population group, costs associated with their care). Successful website designers spend time doing research on who will likely use their website, and why, before defining the features of the website. Organizations should first understand and identify the audiences they desire to target through their digital health activation efforts.

Long used in other industries, a growing number of healthcare organizations are applying market segmentation techniques to their population health efforts in order to gain "economies of scale". Market segmentation is the process of dividing a broad population into subgroups based on some type of shared characteristic(s). The methods used to divide patient population groups can range from the simplistic (e.g. segmenting by age or gender) to the advanced use of statistical computation programs (e.g. cluster analysis). There is no universally accepted segmentation of persons/consumers with a myriad of approaches designed to achieve varied purposes. The most obvious approach is to leverage demographic dimensions such as gender, age, and race. Although these dimensions are important, they usually provide little understanding about how and why persons/consumers go about selecting and using healthcare services.

A more sophisticated person/consumer segmentation approach is to analyze past known encounter data from the organization's web traffic, electronic health record (EHR) system and/or billing system, with known external behavior, consumer, and geospatial data. Carolinas HealthCare System (CHS), a large healthcare provider organization operating throughout North and South Carolina, employed such an approach using data from their 2.2 million patients.[1] By using a sophisticated hierarchical cluster analysis, CHS was able to sort their patients into seven mutually exclusive groups.

B. Embrace an Activation Approach

There are several approaches organizations can use to guide the digital health activation of their targeted audience(s). Below are some of the most common (and perhaps most effective) approaches.

Emphasize Patient Ownership: Emphasize that it is the patient, not the clinician or healthcare organization, who oversees the patient's health.

Identify Small Steps: Identify small, feasible steps patients can take toward healthier behaviors. Small steps can be used to avoid overwhelming patients and to set them up to succeed in order to take larger steps in the future.

Incentives: Take a page out of the consumer marketing playbook and use incentives for patients to take specific actions. Offering giveaways, rewards, or donations in exchange for desired behaviors are all strategies available for healthcare organizations to consider.

---

[1] Butcher, L. (2016, March 8). Consumer Segmentation Has Hit Health Care. Here's How It Works. Hospitals & Health Networks.

2. *Strategies for Engaging Patients*

Having activated patients is one thing. Sustaining the activated behavior is another, and perhaps a more challenging task. Yet is a critical component to realizing the outcome benefits of patient empowerment.

As presented in the earlier chapters, there is a plethora of digital health tactics and technologies organizations could offer patients in order to empower them in their care. But instead of starting with those tools and then looking to see how to change behaviors, perhaps healthcare organizations should begin with the science of behavior change. While there are several psychological frameworks that can be leveraged to support sustained health behavior change, chief among these are goal setting approaches.

To make sure patient activation/engagement goal setting is done effectively as part of web design, it is useful to begin with the psychological principles behind goal setting. These guiding principles can help web teams in the design of a digital health behavior change website.

A. *Set the Right Kinds of Goals*

Setting a healthcare website up for success means providing the right kind of goals for the users to set. This can be tougher than it seems as many organizations offer patients tools that ask users to simply select a goal from a list of one-size-fits-all goals. This is problematic since it may enable early failure or even backfire and prove unhealthy.

Instead, effective websites encourage users to set goals that are

Specific and Clear: To enable successful goal setting and completion, website applications need to enable a single, clear goal with concrete steps to achieve that goal.

Attainable: Website users must also believe that they can achieve the goal they've set. They need to have a sense of "self-efficacy". A user who feels they can achieve the goal is more likely to strive for it and persevere than a user who feels the goal is out of their reach.

B. *Acknowledge That Progress Takes Time*

Many people run into problems when they try to change too much, too fast. If unhealthy behaviors develop over the course of time, then why should it come as a surprise that healthy replacement behaviors require time too. When people set goals, many have a conscious or subconscious expectation of seeing "immediate" change and results. When that expectation is not fulfilled, people tend to give up.

Effective websites address the following:

Emphasize That Long-Term Commitment Is Critical: For a goal-oriented web application to be successful, it is critical to get the user to commit to a long-term effort and acknowledge that change may be slow. By setting the correct type of expectations, and asking for explicit commitment, the provider organization is enabling the user to alter their emotional responses to slow early progress and helps them stay engaged for longer.

Track Progress and Celebrate Milestones: Given that it takes time to change behavior, not seeing rapid progress can be frustrating and demotivating to many. Small, incremental goals and wins help people stay motivated through the process of behavior change. When designing reward systems for goal setting applications, provider organizations need to reward the hard work and small steps achieved, and not just successful change or the end goal.

Manage Failure: A huge barrier to achieving goals is the fear of failure. If a person fails to meet a weekly goal, they are much less inclined to continue pursuing their goal. Designing website applications that acknowledge failure to reach a goal and then reengaging the user is a difficult but necessary process. Streaks, for example, are a commonly used form of reinforcement for engagement, but when someone breaks a streak by missing a day, it can be demotivating. Web designers need to acknowledge the probability of these situations occurring and design for failure events.

Support Autonomy and Adaptation: If a goal has not been reached (for example, if it was an unrealistic goal), the program should offer users the autonomy to change their goals to a more realistic one and recommit to trying it. These events should be framed in a supportive and positive way, so that users feel enabled to restart with a fresh mind-set.

Summary

Patient engagement is widely recognized as being critical to many positive outcomes for patients and society. Healthcare provider organizations are to be commended for leveraging their organization's resources, including their website, for patient engagement purposes. While much of a provider's website functions to empower patients, the utility of digital health tools is useless unless patients use the resources offered to them. Stimulating patients to take some desired action (Patient Activation) and then encouraging the continuation of that behavior (Patient Engagement) need to be part of a provider's calculus when developing a strategy for the organization's website. As outlined in this chapter, there are several different approaches and strategies organizations should consider.

Discussion Questions

1. In your own words, describe the difference between "patient empowerment", "patient activation", and "patient engagement".
2. For digital health Patient Activation to occur, organizations must know the specific patient being activated. Looking through the HEWSi™ model, where would you begin Patient Activation management and measurement efforts? Explain your answer.
3. Search a healthcare provider organization's website and describe their approach for activating patients. Discuss your assessment of their approach.
4. Create a digital health Patient Engagement goal for yourself and explain why you believe it is "specific" and "attainable".

Appendix:
HEWSi™ Instrument

Function Measures

Does the Website...

ORIENTING			
Access			
Primary Points of Contact	List the following points of contacts:		
	• Hours of operation and/or visitation hours?	Yes ◯	No ◯
	• Main fax number?	Yes ◯	No ◯
	• Main phone number?	Yes ◯	No ◯
	• Physical address?	Yes ◯	No ◯
	• Primary email address (for inquiries)?	Yes ◯	No ◯
Service-Specific Contacts	Include contact information for some/all available clinical services to include:		
	• Hours of operation and/or visitation hours?	Yes ◯	No ◯
	• Main fax number?	Yes ◯	No ◯
	• Main phone number?	Yes ◯	No ◯
	• Physical address?	Yes ◯	No ◯
	• Primary email address (for inquiries)?	Yes ◯	No ◯

(Continued)

ORIENTING (*Continued*)			
Wayfinding	Include a visual map of:		
	• The health campus in relationship to the surrounding area (e.g. cross-streets, markers)?	Yes ○	No ○
	• The interior of the health campus?	Yes ○	No ○
	• The organization's geographical coverage/area of influence?	Yes ○	No ○
Identification			
Brand Consistency	Reflect the provider organization's brand guidelines (colors, font, etc.)?	Yes ○	No ○
Identification Statement	Include a statement indicating that the provider organization endorses the content on the website?	Yes ○	No ○
Name and Logo	Have the name and/or official logo of the provider organization appear on all main pages of the website?	Yes ○	No ○
Website URL	URL reflect the corporate name of the provider organization in some form or fashion?	Yes ○	No ○
Leadership			
Leadership Team	List the leaders of the organization and their role/function?	Yes ○	No ○
Leadership Team Profile	Include a biographic profile of the leaders of the organization?	Yes ○	No ○
Primary Leader	Identify the primary leader of the provider organization (e.g. CEO, Board Chairperson)?	Yes ○	No ○
Primary Leader Message	Include a welcome message to web visitors from the organization's primary leader?	Yes ○	No ○
Primary Leader Profile	Include a biographic profile of the organization's primary leader?	Yes ○	No ○

ORIENTING (Continued)			
Organizational Story			
Mission, Vision, and Values	Include the provider organization's:		
	• Mission statement? A mission statement communicates the organization's reason for being, and how it serves its key stakeholders.	Yes ◯	No ◯
	• Vision statement? A vision statement is a future-oriented pronouncement of the organization's aspirations.	Yes ◯	No ◯
	• Key values? Values are the emotionally invested principles guiding the organization in realizing their mission and vision.	Yes ◯	No ◯
Organization History and Milestones	Include a summary profile of the organization's history and/or key moments?	Yes ◯	No ◯
Payment			
Payment Process	Provide an overview of the payment process?	Yes ◯	No ◯
Payment Resources	Provide users with contact information for those with payment questions/concerns?	Yes ◯	No ◯
Payment Responsibilities	Explain (at some level of detail) patient responsibility in paying for the services rendered?	Yes ◯	No ◯
Payment Sources	List the varied payment sources accepted?	Yes ◯	No ◯
Performance			
Clinical Quality	Contain current (less than one year old) measures of the organization's clinical care performance (e.g. surgery complications)?	Yes ◯	No ◯
Community Involvement	Profile the organization's assessment of and/ or involvement in supporting the care needs of at-risk communities (e.g. community needs assessment, charity care)?	Yes ◯	No ◯
Complaints	Address how users can register a complaint about the organization's services?	Yes ◯	No ◯

ORIENTING (*Continued*)			
External Recognition	List of the organization's awards/ certifications?	Yes ○	No ○
Patient Satisfaction	Provide patient satisfaction:		
	• Measures that are no more than a year old?	Yes ○	No ○
	• Survey/analytical methodological description?	Yes ○	No ○
Performance Improvement	Address how the organization has used patient complaints and/or clinical quality measures to improve the organization's services?	Yes ○	No ○
Real-Time Informing			
Current Wait Time	Provide the current average wait time for select clinical services (e.g. Emergency Department, Urgent Care)?	Yes ○	No ○
Webcam	Provide a real-time video feed of select areas of the campus (e.g. parking lot) to help prepare patients when accessing the organization's services?	Yes ○	No ○
Services/Providers			
Clinical Practitioner Directory	List the clinical practitioners formally associated with the provider organization?	Yes ○	No ○
Clinical Practitioner Profile	Provide some level of information on the clinical practitioner(s) associated with the provider organization (e.g. schools attended, board certifications)?	Yes ○	No ○
Clinical Services Description	Provide some level of detail describing and/ or explaining the clinical services available at the provider organization?	Yes ○	No ○
Clinical Services Directory	List the clinical services available at the provider organization?	Yes ○	No ○

Does the Website...

ENLIGHTENING			
Care Environment			
Advanced Clinical Services Description	Provide a more than cursory description of the clinical services offered by the provider organization?	Yes ○	No ○
Community/Social Services Directory	Provide a listing of local health/social service organizations and events?	Yes ○	No ○
Local/National/ International Health News	Provide access to a health news resource?	Yes ○	No ○
Clinical			
Complementary and Alternative Medicine (CAM)	Provide information related to complimentary and/or alternative medicine?	Yes ○	No ○
Generalized Clinical Information	Provide access to generalized clinical information related to various pathological conditions?	Yes ○	No ○
Self-Assessment Tools	Provide access to generalized clinical (self-administered) risk assessment tools/tests?	Yes ○	No ○
Experiential			
Patient Advocacy Services	Provide information on patient advocacy services (e.g. dealing with insurance or navigating the system)?	Yes ○	No ○
Patient Rights	Provide some statement about the rights of patients?	Yes ○	No ○
Patient Stories	Provide patient experience stories?	Yes ○	No ○

Does the Website...

ALIGNING			
Resource Alignment			
Membership Programs	Offer website visitors the ability to join a provider-sponsored health membership program?	Yes ◯	No ◯
Philanthropic— Information	Provide website visitors information about donating to the organization?	Yes ◯	No ◯
Philanthropic— Portal	Offer website visitors an online portal to donate financially to the organization?	Yes ◯	No ◯
Products/Services	Offer website visitors the ability to purchase items (e.g. purchase flowers, car seats, "swag") or services (e.g. care sitters) through an online store?	Yes ◯	No ◯
Intimacy			
External Social Media	Allow website visitors the ability to publicly share their experiences via popular social media tools (e.g. Facebook, Twitter)?	Yes ◯	No ◯
Internal Social Media	Allow website visitors the ability to share their experiences, concerns, and suggestions privately to the provider organization's leaders through an email or electronic form?	Yes ◯	No ◯
Talent Alignment— Employment	Allow website visitors the ability to search and apply for employment opportunities with the provider organization?	Yes ◯	No ◯
Talent Alignment— Volunteer Info	Provide website visitors information on volunteer opportunities with the provider organization?	Yes ◯	No ◯
Talent Alignment— Volunteer Portal	Allow website visitors the ability to apply for volunteer opportunities with the provider organization?	Yes ◯	No ◯
Targeted Behavioral Change	Promote specific desired health behaviors (e.g. smoking cessation, breastfeeding) and offers connections to programs/offerings designed to assist in adopting the promoted desired health behaviors?	Yes ◯	No ◯

Does the Website...

PERSONALIZING			
Empower Access to Information			
Billing Information	Allow patients to view their bill?	Yes ○	No ○
Clinical Information (Download)	Allow patients to download their electronic health record (EHR)?	Yes ○	No ○
Clinical Information (View)	Allow patients to view their EHR?	Yes ○	No ○
Clinical Trial Records	Allow patients to view records involving any clinical trials in which they participate?	Yes ○	No ○
Discharge/Care Instructions	Allow patients to view their discharge/care instructions?	Yes ○	No ○
Diagnostic Images/ Video	Allow patients to view diagnostic images and/or video?	Yes ○	No ○
EHR Integrated with Personal Health Record (PHR)	Allow patients to view the data from the provider organization's EHR with the patient's complete pan-organizational PHR via one viewer or presentation method?	Yes ○	No ○
Immunizations (Public Health)	Allow patients to view their immunization record from external national registries?	Yes ○	No ○
Patient Demographics	Allow patients to view their patient profile?	Yes ○	No ○
Empower Access to Tools			
Assessment/Tracking Tools			
Condition-Specific Self-Management Tools	Provide patients access to condition-specific tracking and reporting tools?	Yes ○	No ○
Symptom Assessments	Provide patients with clinically accepted reliable tools that allow them to report symptom outcomes?	Yes ○	No ○
Planning Tools			
Advance Care Plan	Provide patients with a tool that helps them detail their advance care plan?	Yes ○	No ○

PERSONALIZING (Continued)			
Care Comparisons	Provide patients with a tool that allows them to objectively compare healthcare providers?	Yes ○	No ○
Preventive Services	Provide patients with select preventive care planning tools?	Yes ○	No ○
Wellness Plan	Provide patients with a tool that helps them develop a plan of action geared towards achieving personal wellness goals?	Yes ○	No ○
Post-Encounter Tools			
Care Experience Surveys	Allow patients to rate their care experience?	Yes ○	No ○
Care Reminders	Allow patients to receive alerts, reminders, and notifications about care plan activities?	Yes ○	No ○
Community Health Programs	Allow patients to enroll in community health improvement initiatives?	Yes ○	No ○
Online Patient Payments	Allow patients to pay online any charges they may have incurred in the course of their treatment?	Yes ○	No ○
Service Requests— Appointments	Allow patients to schedule an appointment?	Yes ○	No ○
Service Requests— Prescription Refills	Allow patients to request prescriptions be refilled by the provider's pharmacy?	Yes ○	No ○
Empowering Control			
Medical Records Privileges			
Grant Access Permissions (EHR)	Allow patients to designate who (beyond the care team) can view their medical record?	Yes ○	No ○
Record Correction Requests	Allow patients to request corrections to their medical record?	Yes ○	No ○
Set Privacy Controls	Allow patients to restrict what information in the medical record external parties can view?	Yes ○	No ○

PERSONALIZING (Continued)			
Transmit Patient Record (Electronically)	Allow patients to initiate the electronic distribution of their patient record to whomever they desire?	Yes ○	No ○
Pan-Organizational PHR Privileges			
Grant Access Permissions (pan-org PHR)	Allow patients to designate who (beyond the care team) can view their medical record?	Yes ○	No ○
Optimizing Empowerment			
e-Consultations			
e-Visits	Allows patients to have asynchronous online medical consultations with their healthcare provider?	Yes ○	No ○
Online Health Professional	Allows patients the ability to chat online with a healthcare professional (e.g. nurse, social worker) about health concerns?	Yes ○	No ○
Preferred Language	Allow patients to have e-consultations in their preferred language?	Yes ○	No ○
Secure Messaging	Allow patients/providers the ability to exchange patient health information to one another via a secure and encrypted platform?	Yes ○	No ○
Virtual Coaching	Allows patients the ability to access virtual coaching services?	Yes ○	No ○
Patient-Generated Health Data (PGHD) Services			
Remote Patient Monitoring	Allows patients to submit and access PGHD?	Yes ○	No ○

Form Measures

Does the Website...

STRUCTURAL ISSUES IMPACTING WEBSITE USERS			
Accessibility			
Audio			
Audio Controls	Allow website visitors to control the audio (e.g. pause, stop, change the volume) of any audio files used in the website independent of the audio controls of the device used to access the website?	Yes ○	No ○
Audio Description	Allow auditory-only information to be communicated via alternative mediums?	Yes ○	No ○
Browser Compatibility			
Browser Compatibility	Provide content that can be interpreted reliably by a wide variety of popular browsers?	Yes ○	No ○
Compliance			
Disability Compliance	Comply with applicable federal and local regulations governing website accessibility for individuals with disabilities?	Yes ○	No ○
Manual			
Animation Control	Allow website visitors to manage the tempo (e.g. stop, adjust) of animated web content?	Yes ○	No ○
Interactive Content	Allow website visitors to manage the tempo (e.g. stop, adjust) of web content in which user interaction is limited by time?	Yes ○	No ○
Keyboard Control	Allow website visitors to control all functionalities of the website using a keyboard?	Yes ○	No ○
Keyboard Navigation	Allow website visitors to navigate through the entire website using a keyboard?	Yes ○	No ○

STRUCTURAL ISSUES IMPACTING WEBSITE USERS *(Continued)*			
Software Tools			
Data Entry	Instruct users how to correctly input data and correct a data entry error after a data entry error alert is issued?	Yes ○	No ○
Data Entry Errors	Alert users when an error occurs in the entry of data, identifying the wrong element, describing the error, and offering a solution?	Yes ○	No ○
Definition Tool	Provide a tool to define specific words, phrases, acronyms, and/or abbreviations?	Yes ○	No ○
Discoverable Language	Allow the default language of each web page to be detected by browser software programs?	Yes ○	No ○
Pronunciation Tool	Provide a tool to help visitors pronounce specific words or phrases?	Yes ○	No ○
Visual			
Contrast Ratio Color	Use a contrast ratio color of at least 4.5:1 for texts and images?	Yes ○	No ○
Image Descriptions	Provide text descriptions for all nontext content?	Yes ○	No ○
Photosensitivity	Avoid the use of visual media involving flashes or changes of luminosity that may cause damage or alterations to a viewer's health?	Yes ○	No ○
Subtitles	Provide subtitles or audio descriptions for all audible content?	Yes ○	No ○
Text to Speech	Allow text to be read by text-to-speech software programs?	Yes ○	No ○
Confidentiality-Privacy			
Confidential Statement	Provide clear information about its privacy and confidentiality policy?	Yes ○	No ○
Data Management	Provide users information on how to manage personal information data concerns?	Yes ○	No ○

STRUCTURAL ISSUES IMPACTING WEBSITE USERS (*Continued*)			
User Protections	Provide clear information about protections extended to users in the collection of data?	Yes ◯	No ◯
Target Audience			
Audience Adaptation	Curate its content for varied audiences?	Yes ◯	No ◯
Audience Identification	Identify to whom its contents are directed?	Yes ◯	No ◯
Usability			
Health Literacy			
Acronym Definition	Define acronyms and abbreviations in their first appearance on each web page?	Yes ◯	No ◯
Acronym Use	Avoids/limits the use of acronyms and abbreviations?	Yes ◯	No ◯
Medical Terms	Define the medical terms used in the website?	Yes ◯	No ◯
Multilingual	Allow website visitors to view website content in other languages?	Yes ◯	No ◯
Readability	Use words that are simple and understandable by the targeted audience(s)?	Yes ◯	No ◯
Textual Brevity	Avoid using more words than necessary?	Yes ◯	No ◯
Labeled			
Titles and Headers	Web pages use titles and headers to help organize website content?	Yes ◯	No ◯
Legibility and Visual Design			
Font Size	Instruct how and/or offer a tool to adjust web page font sizes?	Yes ◯	No ◯
Font Style	Use a font style that makes text easily visible, distinguishable, and recognizable by the majority of visitors?	Yes ◯	No ◯

STRUCTURAL ISSUES IMPACTING WEBSITE USERS (Continued)			
Printable	Allow content to be printed without losing legibility?	Yes ○	No ○

Navigation

Breadcrumb Navigation	Provide a graphical navigational aid allowing users to keep track and maintain awareness of their location in the website which is visible and accessible on all pages of the site?	Yes ○	No ○
External Link Alert	Alert website visitors when they are being redirected to content/webpages outside the current website?	Yes ○	No ○
Identifiable Links	Present easily identifiable web page hyperlinks?	Yes ○	No ○
Primary Menu	Display the main navigation menu clearly and accessibly on all pages of the site?	Yes ○	No ○
Search Engine	Offer an internal search engine that is accessible from all pages of the site?	Yes ○	No ○
Secondary Menu	Display a secondary navigation system (e.g. site map, table of contents, keyword indexes) clearly and accessibly on all pages of the site?	Yes ○	No ○
Understandable Links	Clearly explain the purpose of embedded web page hyperlinks?	Yes ○	No ○

Organization of Contents

Continuity	Present a consistent design throughout the entire website?	Yes ○	No ○
Logical Flow	Present content in a logically progressive and easily understandable manner?	Yes ○	No ○
Succinct	Avoid overloading website visitors with an excessive amount of content?	Yes ○	No ○

Does the Website...

STRUCTURAL ISSUES IMPACTING CONTENT MANAGEMENT			
Content Credibility			
Accessing Content Authors/Owners	Provide target audiences a means by which to access those responsible for the website's content?	Yes ○	No ○
Content Criteria	Describe the selection criteria used when external information sources are referenced?	Yes ○	No ○
Content Datedness	Identify the date of the last revision made to each web page?	Yes ○	No ○
Content Sources	Identify the information sources used to populate the website's content?	Yes ○	No ○
Identification of Content Authors/ Owners	Identify those responsible for website content?	Yes ○	No ○
eCommerce			
eCommerce	Detail the terms and conditions regarding the buying and selling of goods or services on the organization's website?	Yes ○	No ○
Editorial Policy			
Advertising	Describe its policy regarding advertising?	Yes ○	No ○
Limitations	Describe the limitations of the information provided on the website?	Yes ○	No ○
Restrictions	Describe the conditions or general restrictions on the use of the information on the website?	Yes ○	No ○
Support	Identify the level of commitment the healthcare organization has, to answer inquiries posed by website users?	Yes ○	No ○
Veracity	Identify the healthcare organization's level of support regarding the veracity of the information provided on the website?	Yes ○	No ○

STRUCTURAL ISSUES IMPACTING CONTENT MANAGEMENT (*Continued*)			
Transparency and Honesty			
Financing and Sponsorship	Provide information about its funding as well as potential conflicts of interest of those with responsibility over the website's content?	Yes ○	No ○
Purpose and Objectives	Describe its purpose and objectives?	Yes ○	No ○

Index